Never Give Up

My life story from Uganda to Iona

By
Doreen Nyamwija

Cloister House Press

First published in the United Kingdom in 2017 by The Cloister House Press

ISBN 978-1-909465-65-7

FOREWORD

Doreen Nyamwija, otherwise known as Dora, is a woman of the world: her experience stradles continents, her enthusiasm and empathy are unbounded, and her faith is transparent and all-inclusive.

Coming from Uganda, a country not famed for good governance or tolerance, she represents a kinder face of her nation, perhaps because her early days acquainted her with difference, limited means and a lack of privilege – the kind of soil which raises people who see life more in terms of blessing than entitlement.

Any who met her in the periods when she was working in Iona will never forget her - her ability to get people singing while doing manual tasks, her delight in dancing whether freestyle or coordinated. Young people will remember her for her pranks, and a special few will remember the magic of the moment when, in tribute to the woman who anointed Jesus with precious ointment, Dora - in a Holy Week service – walked the length of the Abbey church with a flask of perfume balanced on her head.

Marvellously, though she loves Britain and its people, her affection for her own country calls her back for marriage, for charitable work and for the unknown things which God has in store for her.

In this book you will find cameos of her life so far which will enlighten, encourage and challenge. We who have known her pray that the kindness she has shown and shared here will surround her in the next stage of her journey.

John L. Bell
The Iona Community

CONTENTS

I dedicate this book to all of those who have helped me, in different ways while I am on this life journey. Especially my biological mother Eva Agaba, my mum Annie Feeley and Danny Feeley, my Tom, brother Derrick, my nephew Noble Derrick, all my friends, Iona family and Ugandan current and future family.

INTRODUCTION

This life is a journey, and to a girl born in a small village, Mbarara, South West Uganda, this journey has been full of wonders. It has changed me in so many ways that I would never have dreamt of.

When I started to write about my life, I did not know exactly what I wanted to write, but I hoped that someday someone would enjoy reading it, and probably learn something. Even if it gives a little glimpse of hope to someone out there, that would be great.

Quite often we would all like to do something helpful, or even to change the world, but because there is so much to take in, it gets overwhelming and we end up not attempting to do anything at all. This would possibly be the case if I thought too much about how my story may influence the people who read it. I do not even have the equipment I need, or enough English. However, the glass is always "half full" if we choose to look at it that way. As someone who is often described as optimistic, looking at the good in all situations, tonight I have taken the courage to start writing down my story.

It is the 4th of November 2016, and a year from now I hope to be married to Tom my long-time friend and love who is in Uganda now.

Before I go forward to any future, I would like to share an affirmation that I wrote a few months ago to encourage people not to ignore doing the things that seem small, and are in their reach, because I know that "small seeds sometimes grow into mighty trees".

"You do not have to change the whole world in a day, but you could make a difference"

For me this means that:

We should not wait until we are able to feed all the hungry children, people in Africa, South America, Asia or even Glasgow, but we can start now, by sharing the food we have with each other.

We should not wait for immigration and border laws to change, but we can start now by opening our own homes to friends and even strangers.

We should not wait for the whole world to stop discrimination, hatred, violence, oppression but we can start here and now through loving and accepting ourselves and neighbours.

We should not wait to serve God in heaven but we can start here and now through serving those we meet in our daily lives.

This has helped me to understand that I can start from doing just what I can, and sometimes along the way, even what seems impossible could be achieved. I hope this speaks to you too.

Tough times help us to grow stronger. Take a breath, and think exactly what you need to do in this moment, to stay focussed and positive. People always carry something good in them, even when we go off the track, or do the wrong thing, there is something good about each one of us, if we strive to see it, we can see it.

CHAPTER ONE

EARLY DAYS GROWING UP IN UGANDA

My brother Derrick and I started our studies at Tukore Primary School, where my mother was a teacher of deaf pupils for several years. My mother cooked for us, and often while we waited for the food, she taught us a song we could sing to her as she cooked. I was a very picky eater, my mother once told us a story that way back before I could even speak, she spent several days wondering what on earth I wanted to eat as I refused almost everything that was given to me, until she prepared mushrooms and ghee; then I ate so much and she was surprised. I can say that still, I am not fussy, if you cook or give me what I like!

I had a great childhood, we were poor but had enough for our basic needs, and had lots of children to play with in school. We skipped the rope, played hide and seek, omwepena (played with a small ball, made from banana fibres) and it did not matter if one of the students was deaf, because we all knew basic sign language and could easily communicate. Actually, most of my friends were the deaf pupils who were around the same age as me, and there were bigger girls who loved to look after us and carry us on their backs. We would also ride in the wheelchairs. Although it was a school, we lived like a big family.

Every morning before classes we had a school parade, we would sing the school anthem, say morning prayers, sing a few songs too. We queued in order of our heights and classes. The school prefects and teachers on duty would go around checking whether our teeth, uniform and hair were clean. If they were not, you would be punished. It was the same if you arrived late for school. This was harder for those who had to do domestic chores first and then walk long distances to school.

We had so much fun with school friends; we fetched firewood together, went to the same Sunday school and carried water from the borehole. Carrying water from the borehole was a challenge to most of the children with disabilities. Once I was at the borehole with one of the pupils called Matovu who could not pump the borehole on his own, and neither could I since I was young and not strong enough, however jointly we pumped the borehole and both of us got enough water to take back home, he thanked me so much. I must have been 7 years old by then but when he said, "may God bless you" I can still hear those words as if it was yesterday. He appreciated it so much and part of me must have understood that helping, and being appreciated, meant a lot even at that tender age, therefore wished I could help more whenever I could.

When we were small, Derrick and I had to be put to bed in the afternoons so that we did not fall asleep during supper, which we often had very late in the night. I did not like this at the time, but now, if I have the chance to sleep in the afternoon, is very much appreciated. I remember once we almost set the house on fire trying to smoke the matchboxes, which we had taken as a kind of game.

It was not easy for my single mother to look after our cousins, school children, us, do her work and also undertake further studies as a teacher. I recall hearing her say to us, "I wish you could at least learn to wash your own feet"; I suppose she meant that would be at least one less chore for her to do. I admire my mother so much, having lost her husband three years after marriage, and having to take on lots of roles at an early age; she was only 23 years old, even younger than I am right now.

Life was not always easy for my mother. Just after my father died, she had to go back to the school to work, but was not given permission to take Derrick and me with her, even though we were very little. This was because my aunts thought that she would run away with another man, and also because they were angry, and claimed that she had infected their brother with AIDS. My mother never told us all of this, but I learned it from other people. She did not want to make us dislike our aunts, she was always nice to them even knowing all of this. This helped me to forgive them later, after I had discovered that she was not treated very well. Who was I not to forgive them when the person they had hurt most had forgiven them. I also learned to always leave people to make their own judgements about others; to distinguish the mistakes or actions, from the person, and not to tell other people about what someone else did wrong in a way that makes them look like a bad person. Instead, to remember that people are sometimes not just bad, or good, but "they do".

Although my mother spent some time without being able to take us with her to where she worked, with the support of the local council, my grandmother, and Uncle Manzis, she was eventually able to take us to Tukore where she was a teacher.

During the time that we stayed in the village without her, I suffered from malnutrition, and had jiggers (a parasitic sand flea). My aunts could not properly look after us, they had bigger families of their own, were peasants and did not have enough money to support even more children. More so, one of my aunts was separated, the other had lost her husband, therefore they were single parents themselves.

In Tukore we did not have a nanny to look after us, but Naomi, a well behaved deaf student stayed with us, my mother took care of her as she also went to the school, but she looked after us and played with us. The most amazing thing about Naomi was that even if we would normally judge if the food was ready by listening to the water in the food boiling on the cooking stones she always knew when it was ready, without it getting burnt, which was very unusual. Most deaf children could not hear the boiling, so had to wait and smell which was too late, since that meant it would be burning.

We always appreciated that Naomi was also a clean and a well-behaved pupil, she went on to join workshops and learn how to sew when she finished primary 7.

When I was about 6, my brother and I asked my mother to take us to our grandmother for a while so we could stay with her in the village where my late father was born. This meant that we could also spend time with our extended family, cousins and my grandmother whom we would be staying with. It was a wonderful time, we all sat on the floor around which banana leaves were spread and food was careful poured for us to pick it up with our fingers.

My grandmother stayed at the that time in a grass thatched mud hut, which was very beautiful, I wish it still existed, it was nice and round, when it rained the sound of the rain was so musical that it could make you fall asleep as if a lullaby. We shared all basic needs, sometimes even a dose of medication which was supposed to be for one person was shared amongst many. When you finished washing your feet, you would leave the water for the next person then another. The weird thing is that after you had washed your feet, you would spit in it a little before the next person. I wonder now if this was a way of cleansing the water?

The most fun time spent together was fetching firewood and water, carrying it on our heads from a far off well; that is still in existence. This was a good way of interacting with neighbours who would join with us as we went to do some of these chores, especially washing the clothes by the well. We would also meet others on the way.

Gardening was also usually communal, especially harvesting of millet and maize. Normally, young children would stay at home looking after each other and playing games, or sometimes would play games in the garden as the adults did the harvesting. Food was either cooked from homes the night before, or cooking stones were put together in the garden and it was prepared there. This was also a good communal activity as different families would go together and harvest from the garden of one family whose millet was ready for harvest, then go on to another family and another, until they had been around all the homes. However, a lot of gossiping and catching up also took place, as you can imagine.

My grandmother looked after us and several other cousins, she always welcomed people, and greeted everyone with a long lasting traditional hug. She also kept her secret tea with sugar, which we all of course liked so much because we did not have sugar often, unless it was special occasion or we had visitors around. She also always had roasted groundnuts and occasionally shared them with us. Granny Joyce is such a lovely lady, the only time I ever had heard her raise her voice, was when she was talking to her cat. She is a cat lover though, and has always had a cat in her house.

The time came however when my mother decided to take us to a boarding school because it was better academically, and, she would then get enough time to do her job, and look after the special needs children and deaf pupils who had become like her own children.

Before I move to something more than early childhood however, there are few things I did, that I wish I had not done, or could have done better. However, in such instances, I always tried to learn lessons and move on. Such moments however have shaped me to the person I am today.

There was a time I desperately wanted to go and visit my grandmother, to stay with my cousins playing games visiting different aunts and uncles. Normally my mother would take us to the village during school holidays as most of the children from the school had gone to their homes and there were not many to play with and usually my mother would be going to do some further studies. However, this time my mother was unable to take us as she was suffering from malaria.

No sooner had my mother recovered from malaria than my brother Derrick got it. I however insisted that I wanted to go to the village. My mother therefore asked one of our neighbours to take me to our grandmother, later that evening though, before we could go, he said he that was not feeling well either. As the situation was getting worse I said, "please get me out of here before I also get malaria". I wonder if it was because I was too sad to watch both my mother and brother ill, or if just desperately wanted to be in the village?

My mother decided to honour my inconsiderate demands and take us to the village. However on our way, as soon as we had arrived in the town centre, my brother was sick. My mum was not pleased with me, but took me to the taxi park, helped me board a taxi and told the driver and the conductor where to drop me as it was the first time to take such a long journey on my own.

Part of me was excited that I would be going to be with more people friends, cousins, aunts, uncles, but I was also sad to have left in that way and I had, and knew it would not be the same without my brother Derrick. We had grown up like twins, were always together, had arguments, smiles, tears, fights but stayed close. Derrick was born a twin, and though his twin sister Daphne had died when she was very young, most people thought Derrick and I were twins even though he was 2 years older than me. My mother would try to explain but sometimes she did not bother when people said are these your twins she would often nod to say "yes" as I assume she was tired of explaining something which I would imagine was quite sad; "No Derrick's twin died and Dora was born two years later blah blah..."

Fortunately, I got out at the right stop but everyone was surprised that my mother had let me take this journey on my own. Sometimes I think this prepared me to be independent, take my first journey abroad on my own later when I was 18 years old.

The other thing that happened at this time, something that I am not proud of, was that my mother asked me to take the bucket that she had been sick into outside, and I refused. Part of me wants to try and understand why a young girl whose mother had sacrificed so much for, could not do the least she could ask of her, "take her bucket?" I was young, probably scared of what the reaction of my friends would be if I told them I had taken a bucket of sick outside. They might have teased me, been disgusted or made fun of me. As I said, I learned from my actions, my mother never punished me, or told me off for pulling a disgusted face when she was not feeling well, but I learned from it as I grew older and promised myself that I would always clean up anything, and I have probably cleaned sick, spit, poo – you name it. This may also explain why I have never found it disgusting, because I learned that if I think it needs cleaning, and it is disgusting, I am the person to clean it. I do not even pull that face any more.

The holiday before we joined Mbarara Junior School, which was a boarding school, I had been selected to join AEE (which was an organisation that sponsored orphans to go to school). They also bought us scholastic materials, paid fees and we met for annual conferences and were given Christmas gifts too.

Derrick was excited and was also was looking forward to joining Mbarara Junior School. Little did we know that when I had met with staff from the school, this had actually just been on the site/venue for the conference, and therefore the school system, menu, agenda, activities would all be different from that which I had experienced at the conference, and had told Derrick about.

Derrick and I did the pre-entrance interviews, he passed Science and Social studies but did not do as well in Mathematics and English whereas I passed but did not pass Science and Social Studies as well, however as English and Mathematics were seen as the essential subjects, this meant that Derrick would either have to repeat his class Primary 3 instead of joining Primary 4, but because my mother did not want us to stay in the same class, he had to go even further behind to Primary 2 (she thought that this would be dangerous for a girl to do as girls, she felt, were more prone to behave differently during adolescence) and my mother did not want me to be in a lower class when I would be older, as this could involve bullying from older boys, or questions for myself too.

Normally siblings would be in classes relative to their age, so this put my brother at a disadvantage, always having questions from people, "how come your younger sister is in a class higher than yours?" they would assume I was smarter which was not true. It was good enough, because my mother was named as a lady who gave birth to twins; sometimes people never bothered him as much because they thought I was the older one and we did not care to explain.

My brother was disappointed to learn that the school was not as I had explained it during my stay at the conference. In his case he, with the other children, had to clean the dormitories, and toilets (masaka), and had the same food: posho and beans twice a day, compared to all the different kinds of food I had had at the conference. They had to be forced to shower twice a day (he hated it), and hated even more to wake up early in the morning to read (prep).

My mother, even with the support from AEE, could not afford for us both to stay as boarders at the school, but she did want us to be in the same school, so she asked one of the caretakers (the matron) to let me stay with her at the cost of someone who would be commuting. We also ate the same food, but occasionally had a change. Visiting day was the day every child looked forward to, most of us started counting the number of days left to visiting day a few days after our arrival. It was a big disappointment if you did not get visited. I still remember a few children who were sponsored by the TASO, (they were like a family) who came from different families, who had lost their parents to AIDS, a big lady would come on a very loud motor cycle and visit all of them.

I learned so many things from attending this school; washing dishes, clothes, ironing, cleaning, I did more than I had ever done at home. It was very good for my growth. I did not enjoy being beaten though; Sedda who was my caretaker would strike me If I made even the simplest mistake. A slap, considering my size and hers, would blow me to a distance where I would fall down and cry until she pulled me up by grabbing my ears - which was even more painful than the beating.

Before I started the school, I had shared same bed with my mum all my life, this could have been because my father died when I was just one. She did not ever buy a separate bed for me, but there was not much room to add another extra bed anyway. Therefore, I would wake my mother up if I wanted to pee in the night, and she would say to me "yes nothing will harm you I am awake and watching out for you", I trusted my mother and felt protected and safe. Very recently she told me that I would cry every time she left to go somewhere and asked, "will you come back?" Then, when she said "yes", I would just run away to play. Of course, sometimes she would have gone for workshops and not return until the following day or two.

My first few nights with this new caretaker were very frightening. It was not the same as it had been with my mother, I was scared to go to pee on my own when I woke up in the night, so I had a silly idea; I peed on the bed and put a towel between us thinking that maybe she might not notice until the morning. As soon as the urine got close to her however, she noticed. She slapped me so hard that I thought I would faint.

That was not the only incident that I was beaten. Another time, I had woken up after having a nap in the evening, and because we had tea at the same time as our food, I served myself, but being half asleep, I put the beans in my mug instead of tea. There were of course several times that I was beaten, it is so sad that most of the kids, students and children had got used to being hit in their homes, and it became acceptable, almost as if it should be the normal way to discipline children as they grow up. Most teachers and parents seemed to think that if you do not beat children they would misbehave and be spoilt. They justified this by a saying, "spare the rod, spoil the child".

Teachers and parents who beat the children take it as a norm, if you fail a question in class, come to school late, which is very common especially if you commute, and have to first do house chores, bath siblings, pack lunch and then walk miles to school. We were beaten so many times, but one incident I remember well was when I skipped a page in my science book and accidentally wrote on the next new page. When the teacher marked my book, she opened it and noticed there was a space that had not been used. She did not even give me time to explain, I had not even noticed since the pages had been so stuck together. She beat me up so much. This was a human error so I felt treated unjustly, and I think that is why I still remember it.

I hope for a day when parents and teachers will realise that beating children is not the way to work. I plan to undertake talks in schools, as often as I can, to reduce and hopefully stop this practice.

My mother always encouraged me, she knew it was not easy to leave home, come from a village school, where they did not speak much English, or even do enough teaching, to then go to a bigger, and one of the best schools in the district. She would tell me to read and score at least the pass mark 50% so that I would not have to repeat the class. However, she never made me feel stupid, or feel like education was the most important thing. She always told me good behaviour and treating people in a good way was more important.

When I started at the school it was not easy, at one point I scored 7% and had some of my English paper answers read out loud and the rest of the class laughed at me. I can still remember the questions and answers I gave:

Use the following words, "to, too, two" to complete the sentences:

> I have.....................brothers
> I am going................school

As someone who had not had a lot of English lessons, and had most of my lessons explained through our local language in my village school, I assumed of course the answers I needed to fill in would have to be long enough to fit in the long gap left for me to fill so below are my responses:

> I have <u>following</u> brothers
> I am going <u>sentences</u> school

By the end of my final year at this school however, things had turned upside down. I had been confirmed in church, had attended several debates, was voted the head girl and became the best girl in my final year in a class of 145 pupils. By that time, I loved my school, we sang and danced so much, I was in the school choir - even made it to the national level. I remember singing a song about my school, 'I love my school it's for everybody, I never finish up to praise your name; Mbarara Junior is a lovely School'.

Our classes and the teachers were often fun. We had a science teacher for example who told us stories to help us understand, giving us examples for most topics. Some of the examples were quite funny, others rather scary; maybe she used them so that we do not forget them easily. Often these examples would involve her relatives, friends or at least someone she knew, so that it would sound real to us. I am not sure now whether she made them up, but I believed her when we were young; a bit like Santa at Christmas. She told us about her aunt who had leprosy, and as most people in villages used charcoal, and she had no feeling in her hands, she would carry the hot charcoal on her palms from her neighbour's house to their kitchen. Our teacher also said, her aunt would wake up some mornings and find that some of her fingers had dropped off and were lying on her bed.

This teacher would also call us names like "mammals", "vertebrates" for example, so that we would remember them to pass exams.

Derrick and I were very close, we fought, laughed, comforted each other and supported each other.

His friends would come to me at the end of the day, and tell me what funny things he had done or said in class; he has a good sense of humour. Sometimes he would play practical jokes, during the parade or when they were checking for people without a school badge, they missed him because he had used a blue and red pen to draw his own school badge that looked almost like the real one. The teachers later found out about this particular prank, but he was not caned.

Derrick was however not impressed with his younger sister being in a class higher, so he told me that he would work hard to catch up, and if he was given any chance ever to challenge me in academics, he would!

The school held debates, at the end of primary school, my candidate class and Derricks sub-candidate class were competing. He asked me a very difficult question during the debate, which I remember defending myself by saying, "thank you Derrick, I will respond to that when we get home". Everyone thought that was very funny and laughed, so we it ended there and continued with the debate.

Even when we were in different classes, he tried to make sure he got better marks than me, and he usually did.

The annual speech and Parents' Day included singing competitions, drama, and presentations to the best students. However, on one occasion when we were waiting for the class results, there was an outbreak of Ebola in the country so speech day was cancelled. Although disappointed that there were no presentations, we were however happy to learn that we had the same position in class; we were both the 3rd pupil in our respective classes!

Derrick had grown up to be "the man of the house" which is what my mother would refer to him as, and I think sometimes he partly took up the role of being a father, and male role-model to me. There are a few incidences that demonstrate this.

Once we were travelling back home after my mother had picked us from school, she was saving for her further studies and did not have enough money for the transport on her. As we were waiting for a public taxi, my mother having spoken with the conductor explained to us that she had less money than he was asking for, just before the driver could drive off without us, my brother said "mum, stop them here", he pulled out a note, a bit of money he had saved from pocket money in school, and with that we were then able to go home. My mother and I were very impressed.

Also, at the end of Primary school, we were offered an opportunity to go on a trip to the capital city, visit places, like museums, Lake Victoria, the source of the Nile, but I had only half the amount required which our grandmother had given each of us when she had visited, when Derrick heard from his friends that I was not planning to go because of the money, he sacrificed his pocket money for me to join in with the rest of the candidates.

Derrick also wrote to me letters in school encouraging me to "read and study hard". I still remember the words he used just before I sat my final exams. "Prepare, because if you do not prepare, you prepare to fail" He also added, work hard, he based this on the fact that he always thought I was too "laid-back" and that sometimes even when I should be caring, or being serious, I still had what he called "I do not care" attitude, which he told me was good normally, but not for final exams. So, he wrote to me, "the road of 'I do not care', leads to a city of 'had I known'" His words were very powerful and also showed how much he cared for my success.

Derrick taught me so much, he told me that instead of saying "there is not enough food" in case of an unexpected guest, that it's better to drink a lot of water before the meal, so that when we finished the meal, we would be satisfied after eating just a little. This showed me how hospitable he was even at the cost of going with less food.

CHAPTER TWO

SENIOR SCHOOL

Having passed Primary Leaving Examinations with flying colours, I was admitted to the school of my first choice, Bweranyangi Girls School in Bushenyi district.

My mother had gently spoken to us before joining Mbarara Junior School to "always be content, never to steal or admire other people's possessions", she explained that most of the children that we would be studying with were from rich families, and even those who are not, would most of the time at least, have both parents. In our case, she had to be both our mother and father therefore could not afford the luxuries but that she will try and make sure she provides us with the basic needs, and at least bring food whenever she visited.

Bweranyangi was a good school, I had lots of good friends, my cubicle mates were like a family, Hannah, Cathy, Felicia, Jeanette, Julian and I shared almost everything. We polished each other's shoes, fetched water together, helped each other to wake up for morning did prep together and reading. I had lots of other friends outside my dormitory some were as close as sisters I never really had, Tracy, Harriet, Sheila, Edith, and many others, from Bweranyangi. It was proved to me that friends are the family you choose. We shared laugher, tears, success, failures, grew together from being Senior 1 bifobe to grown up candidates.

I lost my grandfather in 2013, it is said that he was over 107 years, I am not sure if this is accurate. He had recorded himself on radio before he died, and we listened to it at the funeral. My favourite memory of him was his evening prayers; we would listen from outside through the window, his prayer was a story of his life, he would mention places he had been to, tough times, joyful times, times when he climbed a tree to escape a serious flood, we would listen till we almost fell asleep since this would take more than 2 hours.

There were tough times, times of loss comforting each other after death of friend's relatives, parent's friends, saying goodbyes through tears and hugs.

Tough times brought us closer. Just before our final examinations, the football team that had been travelling for a competition had a bus accident, we lost our schoolmate and friend Fiona, my friend Rachael who sat next to me in class was also involved and many others. She was in a critical condition, we were all worried, but prayed and stayed positive. She returned after a while to get ready for the final exams, but she could not write with her right hand as a few fragments of glass had been lost in her body after the treatment. We watched her in pain, we did not know if she would manage to sit the exams but fortunately she did.

All the students who had not completed payment for the school fees were sent away a few days before the exams. I knew quite well that my mother did not have the money, the organisation that was paying for me were slow in paying. I did not like the way we were treated, as if it was our fault that we were poor.

Not long after my fees were cleared, Harriet a very generous friend also organised and asked whoever could afford to contribute some money and cleared fees for Sheila who was just about to miss her final Advanced exams.

I loved my school Bweranyangi, I was sure I would be coming back for the higher level, I had even left my pillows and most of my stuff at the school; unlike most students who wanted to go to better schools or schools in the city.

My wish was to go back to Bweranyangi, it had shaped me and made me who I had become, and had made lots of close friends at this school.

However, I had often slept, instead of reading, sometimes we even justified it by saying "God provides to his children even when they are asleep" therefore I did not get high enough results to be admitted back to my school. Most of the other students had passed highly. There had also been a lot of cheating that year, to an extent that the ministry of education communicated through the media that the pass mark would be made higher and also, the marking would be stricter. Those who had nothing to do with cheating mainly read from the balcony of the former art room. We even named it "holy ground" but most of these students worked really hard. They would say, "read as if passing depends only on reading, and pray as if passing depends on only prayer". We even had joint prayers and fasting.

However, I slept more than I did anything else, Florence who was very young, in the 1st year of high school would wake me up with her nice gentle voice: "Doreen please wake up and go to read, you do not even seem like a candidate the rest read so hard, you may fail."

Lots of people were disappointed, a few even told my mother that I must have played, forgotten that I came from a poor family, or had been involved with boys. Many did not think much of me because I had been given a chance to be in one of the best schools in the country so how could I have possibly failed.

One thing I was pleased about though was that towards end of senior 3, I decided I wanted to do the literature class instead of agriculture, this did not go down well with my new literature teacher and she asked how sure I could be to pass a subject that I had not started with the rest after quitting one that I studied since senior one, she dismissed me from all her classes and promised me that I would fail as it needed smart and people who were sure of what they wanted. It was good however that we had two literature teachers, so I attended Miss Ahabwes classes instead and surprisingly, I got good marks for literature, C, which was not bad after being guaranteed to get a failure.

When the results came out however, all you could hear over media was that the senior 4 candidate class year 2006 had cheated, examinations had leaked and due to this the pass mark ratings had all been raised. There was no room for whoever had not been involved, as the marking rates were for across the country and no one would believe that anyone who had a chance to see the exam papers beforehand would not look at them, unless you were a fool, so we were all affected, whether or not we had been involved.

It was sad to say goodbye to friends, even when we knew it would just be for a little while. Tracy had become like a sister, we called each other twins, cried with me and we promised each other that this did not mean the end of our friendship. We sang "Friends Forever".

> As we go on, we still remember,
> all the times we had together,
> and as our lives change (or whatever),
> we will still be friends for ever.

We communicated through our parents' phones during our vacation and prayed we would both be admitted to the same school.

It did not surprise me therefore, when my mother told me recently over the phone, that at Tracy's traditional wedding, she had been treated like a close aunt, or mother. She was even given a big length of African cloth as a present, she likes it too when Tracy calls her "mum".

I spent the vacation following senior 4 with my family, I spent some time working at my mother's school canteen serving pupils and teachers, and it was a good time to catch up with my mum. I also spent some time in the village with my grandmother, listening to her stories, to the radio and doing some gardening in the banana plantations in the morning.

Whilst with my grandmother, I suffered from malaria and was down for a long time. It was not easy to keep in touch with my school friends as there was a poor mobile connection. My grandmother did not have a phone either and I missed having my mums phone to play with.

During the holidays when the Board of Examinations announced that Senior 4 results were out, I went to be with my mother. It was hard to accept that the results I had scored would not let me go back to the school I wanted to be in; my former school Bweranyangi girl's school. I cried for weeks, my mother tried to go back and ask for a vacancy they kept promising her to come the following day and next day then week until she realised it was never going to happen. So many people had scored highly and therefore they would not accept me with my second-grade marks and leave the ones with better marks, I suppose if my mother had been in a higher position, or had enough money, probably that would have happened...you may know the term, "it's who you know".

She therefore went to the school of second choice and luckily enough I had been admitted to it. I, in fact, had no idea which school I had put as my second choice, because at the time we had filled in the forms, I had been so taken by my first choice, that I almost did not care what came after that. I recall asking around whoever had Bweranyangi as first choice to just give me the codes for their 3 other choices and I used these, the same as theirs, since for me the rest of the choices, at that time, did not matter.

My mother tried to explain to me that I could make it anywhere and that I had not failed; but I was not convinced. A few of her friends talked to me too, some in a way that I did not want to hear, but when Monica gently told me that I could make it, even in that school, and gave a few words of advice, I agreed. It was getting rather late waiting around for a school that may never admit me, whereas I had been accepted to another, I therefore agreed to go.

In any case the fees at my former school had increased so much, I do not think my mother would have been able to afford it, whereas at Kibubura my new school now, the fees were still affordable.

I do not usually believe in, or even understand dreams, but a few days before leaving my home to take up the offer of this school I had a dream. I can vaguely recall most of it. In this dream, there was a big house with no single entrance - apart from just a small hole which was on the top of the house, where several people; my mother included, had tried all means to get me into this house. Suddenly, someone came and stopped my mother and said, "you may try, but this is not where I have prepared her to be". I cannot recall the person, if you believe in angels, this would be one, and then I woke up saying to myself "it does not matter what other nice outcomes of going to this new school are, all I want at the moment is to go back to my old school".

Well, I did go in the end. On our way there, we passed Sheila's mum who continued to give me her parental words of wisdom and even gave me a bit of pocket money before I headed off to my new school Kibubura.

To be fair, it was worse than I had even imagined it to be. I cried several times at night, even on the first day one of the teachers told me off for bringing biscuits, and a leather suitcase. She put me in a dormitory that was so close to the kitchen, that the smoke came straight to my bed. She said I had been pampered being in a good school, so this school was meant to make me a stronger lady in the future - did this work I wonder?

I did not like the way they separated older girls, or those in higher classes from those in lower classes, because in my former school I was used to a mixture of all ages and classes where it felt like having older and younger sisters (family). Anyway, perhaps fortunately, there was no room for me in the dormitory for 'A' level students, so I was put with those in lower classes. I loved it and made some life long friends like Gloria, even though they were younger than me. She encouraged me, and told me that I would soon get used to the life at the school and would stop crying and comparing the two different schools.

I soon started getting used to, and even liking the school; I would bring a 5-litre Jerri can of ketchup which we would then share.

The school however had a few major catastrophes, the toilet facilities were so poor that one of the students fell in the pit latrine because it was so old. Nothing was ever done about it, we had to continue using it. The most hurtful thing was that a few teachers made comments like "the more you eat the more you need a toilet", and that perhaps this accident was just "a beginning". We thought that maybe more pit toilets were about to collapse. I was concerned also that they did not care enough for the little child who had fallen in and been covered in poo. It was a kind gentle teacher who eventually brought ladders, after the girl's friend was heard screaming and calling out for help. They then got the girl out of the pit and bathed her. But they did not even take her for further medication, despite all the shivering and scare she had received, she must have been only 12 or 13 years old. Instead they put her in the school sick bay and gave her a few sweets to make bad taste in mouth disappear and perfume to stop the smell.

The students were not happy about this, we asked if she could be taken to hospital, which was later done, but only after a serious student demonstrations and a strike.

We were all sent home after the strike, this was hard especially since parents had to pay for damages, also transport, and because we were beaten by the police. But so many other nice things happened in the school though, sports matches, debates, school trips, discussions, seminars, conferences.

However, in my final year, there was an outbreak of fire. It burnt down a whole dormitory, one of the younger students who was feeling unwell had narrowly escaped, after she had felt the heat coming from beneath her bed. She uncovered herself thinking she was only too hot because she was not feeling well. Another student saved her in the end. We have never known what the cause of this fire that burnt down the dormitory was, but several other schools in the country had fires at the same time. Despite this a few students were blamed and suspended, as they were thought to have set the fire. As students, we were all accused and investigated, which was not actually good timing, since it was a couple of months before our final exams. Because the school had earlier been closed after the strike we therefore had less time to study, and we did not know if we could pass. Soldiers guarded the whole school at night with guns, we were scared to move, we could not even read at night.

I was studying history, economics, literature and divinity, the literature class was small and Ndeba one of our teachers of prose and poetry continuously told us to read the books, to pass. I did not read enough, Hilda who slept on the bed next to mine, read books to me as we sat on our beds, almost in form of a story. This saved me from reading the books myself. We had also watched some of the films like Jane Eyre which helped me to get the context.

Hilda and several of us had lots of discussions to prepare for our final exams; none of us had ever scored better than a grade D.

The thing I hated most about this school though, was the morning reading, (we called them "preps"). This was compulsory, a roll call was carried out, and whoever was missing would be severally punished, either beaten, or given tasks to do like cutting the grass, cleaning toilets. If you missed the preps several times, you could even be suspended from school.

When we were in primary school, we would have to wake up very early in the morning to do domestic chores before heading to school. It was not really that early, but I still found it difficult. Often, our caretaker would wake us up, then we would kneel to say a prayer, most of the times, I fell asleep half way through, then I would hear her calling out my name. I would have no idea when I fell asleep, but I always woke up to finish the prayer, so would say "in the name of our Lord Jesus Christ we pray and believe". I am sure she would know every day that I must have been asleep, but she was one of the most understanding ladies you could meet. All the children, called her Kaka (granny), She had never had children of her own, she treated almost the whole school as if we were her own children. She was disabled, she taught me so much, her name was Matron Vasta, and we all loved her.

I am not a morning person, but had no choice. One day, a teacher (who we called "Doi Doi" because doi, doi, was the sound his cane made) found me sleeping in class one morning, we were all always scared of him, he would normally beat students, never even giving them a chance to explain, or to say anything. One early morning however, he found me and a few others sleeping, he called us out and asked us why we were sleeping, which was a surprise, as normally he would have just beaten us. On that morning though, he gave all of us a chance to speak, asking us why we were asleep in the morning class. I must have been half asleep otherwise I do not know how I would have had the courage to say all this. I told him:

> "I came to class to sleep, I have never come to morning prep to read, I read better during day. I only come to make sure my name is on the roll call, to avoid the consequences. I am a coward, I cannot stay in the dormitory on my own, so that is why I come to class. You can beat me today, tomorrow and another day, but that will not change the fact that I will still sleep in the morning."

The class all laughed, and must have thought that I was insane. He asked me if he should take it further and speak to the head mistress and I said "YES".

Later he said, "all of you can go back to your seats, she has saved you". He never told the headmistress, he did not beat us again for a while, but this practice still goes on.

I hope that one day, young people will not be forced to read so early in the morning. It does work for some, but it is more of a punishment to most people, 5 O'clock in the morning is not a time for most children to be up and reading, especially after going to bed late in the evening due to compulsory night preps.

The break, the vacation before University, was a long one. My mother let me work at her school canteen again. It was then I experienced my first "crush" or the one that I remember from being an adolescent. There was a young guy who came to my mother's school, I cannot even recall his name now, but he had all the physical descriptions we always fantasised about in high school; tall, side burns, lots of hair, great smile, charming, we must have chatted for almost 20 minutes, I never saw him again...

CHAPTER THREE

UNIVERSITY PLANS

When the results were out, we found out that we had all passed. It was also announced on the radio, it had been a long time since my school had got anyone with more than twenty points, Patience was the best with twenty-two, then I followed with twenty-one. My mother, my family, everyone was so pleased; especially because they had not excepted much from a third school choice.

While the school Head Teacher at my mother's school was away, my mother was in her office and helping receive any visitors. It was a very fortunate day for her to meet up with Annie and Danny who were volunteering with VSO at a neighbouring teacher training institution (Bishop Stuart College) and were taking a tour around the school and visiting some of the children with special needs.

Amongst all their conversations, they talked to her about challenges of being a single parent, she later asked them if they knew organisations or charities that would sponsor students through university they said they did not know any, and did not have enough money themselves as they had retired unexpectedly due to unavoidable circumstances, and therefore depended on only their pension which could not be enough to commit themselves to an extra expense of fees. However later they decided to put up a Blog with the information below:

> Danny and I get many requests to sponsor students
> for secondary school or university and since we
> haven't won the lottery and, therefore, can't

sponsor them all, we have chosen a local girl. Doreen Nyamwija is 18 and has recently completed secondary school with good grades. Her mother has been a widow for 18 years and teaches at a school for deaf and disabled children. On a teacher's salary of 200,000 shillings ($100) per month she can't afford to send Doreen to university

Annie kept an update about the funds, my results, and hopes for further studies and occasionally posted pictures of me. By the end of a few weeks, enough money to pay for all my 3 years of university had been contributed by friends and relatives including Aillidh and her sister who were about 6 (family friends), Bill (Danny's long-time friend at the school he was a principal), Cathy (Annie's sister, Christy and Jerry (Annie's sister in law and brother), Annie and Danny also paid for my upkeep and accommodation

It came as a very good surprise to me and my mother when time for looking for university accommodation came; we were trying to look for cheaper ones whereas Annie and Danny wanted the best. We were not quite sure when they agreed to support me, whether I had just been a poor African child they had sponsored tuition for, and that was it, but surprisingly, a bond started to form and before long I had become a part of their international family - Annie is American, Danny is Scottish, and I am Ugandan. They paid for me to stay in one of the best accommodation blocks around the campus. Akamwesi, did all my shopping, it was overwhelming, I could not have asked for more, lovely people, who became my friends, family and cared beyond my imagination.

I could never have imagined all this, except when later my brother found a prayer that I had written as a child, which said that I was praying, and hoping to go to university, even if though I knew my mother could not afford it, "that which no eye has seen, no ear has heard, and no mind has perceived" is what I hoped the Lord would do for me. This definitely became true, I do not quite remember writing that prayer, but indeed a way was made for it to happen, and that somehow is was more than a miracle. Even if my mother had sold all she owned Derrick and I could not have both gone to University, and even if we had, there would not have been enough to pay for the accommodation.

My mother was able to get a loan to pay for Derrick's tuition and she also got some support from Tukore Primary School where she was still working.

I really enjoyed life at University, we went out dancing, visiting friends, and although it could have been a challenge to come from the village and straight into a city, and to have almost everything, I never took all this for granted. I shared as much as I could, and supported my brother back at home too.

It was hard to say goodbye to Annie and Danny as their time in Uganda had come to an end. There were lots of tears, because they had become my second family and I had just joined university. My mother was so far away, how would I manage? I had lots of supportive friends however, and I was adaptable too and this made life easier.

I liked the comforts of being at university, but when I was at home for holidays I never really missed them; the electricity, TV, gas cooker. Everything was different at home, but I suppose that it was just the same as it always had been, so I immediately felt at home and did not even find it difficult without these things. It was as if the gas cooker was for Kampala, and firewood was for home.

University had some challenges, I had done a lot of public speaking way back as a head girl in my primary school, and had been at debates, but I was used to supportive people who did not criticise or judge. This was different at university, there was someone, who despite being my friend, continuously teased me for my poor English and local accent. It started as a joke but then later ended up having a "knock on" effect on my confidence. I remember one occasion where I failed to discuss our course work in front of the whole class. I was representing the whole group, so this meant we would all be affected by my poor performance. However, the lecturer carried on with the discussion as I was brought to tears, I had lost my confidence.

Most people around me knew, and were fluent in English even those in my coursework group but they were nice to me, their response surprised me, because I thought they would hate me for my poor representation of the group.

A few friends also encouraged and told me that I would get better at English. This is one of the things I really like about Iona, people are very supportive. Sometimes it is hard to imagine that I have been able to lead services in front of a big congregation that come from all over the world, also to train, supervise and work alongside volunteers from different countries and a big range of ages. Once I was leading the pilgrimage on Iona, and one of the guests asked me "where do you get your confidence from?" I responded to her that "it is from people". People on Iona are very supportive and encouraging, even when you have done the wrong thing, they often use positive criticism. This is possible everywhere if we all try and learn not to use words to bring down people, words are very powerful and should help to build us up, not bring us down. If it is not a positive comment nor positive criticism, keeping silent is the best option.

After my first year of university, Annie and Danny invited me to visit them in Scotland, I applied for my first visa and it was denied because I had not put enough evidence to show that I would be returning to my country. I tried again, with reference letters (one from the university) and later got my visa.

When I got to the UK border however, I was interviewed for such a long time, everyone from the plane I had travelled on had picked up their bags and gone, and even another plane had landed and they also had disembarked. This left a very worried Annie and Danny in the waiting room, it was my first long trip, they wondered if something had gone wrong, or even if I had even been kidnapped.

The problem was that I did not have any money, or cards with me, I had a 500 Ugandan coin which is worth less than a penny. Finally, I thought of giving them Danny and Annie's mobile phone number, which the officials then used to talk to them in the waiting room. They asked if they accepted responsibility for a girl from Uganda without any money, and how long they had known me etc.

I do not know what changed their minds, but I was happy to finally get out and to get warm hugs and a great welcome from Annie and Danny.

My trip and stay in Scotland was great. Danny taught me how to ride a bike, swim, and we went for several walks in the beautiful countryside. Danny's father had told him earlier as a child, that "this is all your inheritance, a beautiful country."

A bond was created, we even became closer after my visit, I feel blessed to have got a second chance of having a father role model, and more than one mother. We even have family names, Queen duf, Princess duf, and King duf, Annie, Dora, Danny respectively. We are family, together we have fights, tears, laughter and share all special moments. Even my biological mum, calls Annie my other mother, and Annie calls her the same. It's such a special feeling.

Danny also has the same name as my late father Daniel. It is an unbelievable coincidence.

We visited a lot of lovely places, amongst which was Iona (one of the Hebrides Isles in Scotland) and where I am currently working. Annie and Danny had been here for their honeymoon and had described how beautiful it was. As we were visiting, we discovered about the Iona Community. Danny paid for me to be a guest for a week, where there was also a Swedish confirmation group. We were staying at the McLeod centre, we went on the pilgrimage, tried ceilidh dancing, that I enjoyed so much, and a guest concert, I even sang and felt comfortable around these people I hardly knew.

I think I felt so comfortable there because there was a big sense of acceptance and encouragement. No-one "pinned you down" if you did not get it right, and most people told me how lovely it was to hear me sing.

On my way back to Uganda, something went wrong with the plane though. All I recall is a few people falling on the floor, my neighbour however, who was an elderly Indian man did not look as scared as I felt. He seemed to just be in his own little world, so I looked at him reading his book, and with time, I was not paying much attention to what had happened and started to feel calm. We were later told that there had been a technical problem with the plane, which I suppose had to wait until we had safely landed - all this had happened when we were already over Entebbe airport. We were only a few minutes late, but I found my cousins waiting for me; as it had been such an experience, they drove me to their home in Nansana, Kampala where I spent a night before travelling to my home in Mbarara the following day. However, on the route home I also survived a bus accident and by the time I finally got home my mother was covered in tears and shaking; I had called her and told her what had happened whilst we were on the way. Our bus driver had lost both his legs in the accident, and 2 people had died who were in the car that had been crushed by the bus. It was worse because the people who had died had been our immediate neighbours.

Stuck in my memory, is that the bus door got stuck; we had to jump through the window to get out, next to me was a lady about 6 months pregnant - how she ever got out, I do not know. It was scary to jump out of the window only to land on the road. I remember thinking then, "anything can happen". Also, I remember the sight of blood, and a hand which lay in the middle of the road together with a few other body parts. It was quite frightening.

During my trip in Scotland, my favourite time was when we went to Corryvrecan for a boat trip on very serious waves to see the whirlpool which happens in the straights between the islands. I loved the excitement of that. But, after the bus accident everything became scary, I could hardly cross the road on my own, I was scared to be in a fast car, and I did not want to travel as much. I still do not enjoy boat rides as much, and sometimes it is not even easy to be on a choppy ferry across to the island to Iona. It is now six years ago, so I am hoping that it gets better.

I never thought I would go on plane again after that, but I have been a few times since then. However, I can say that I have never felt as safe as I did for my first trip. I am scared, but I do not like fear stopping me from doing what I ought to do, so somewhere I find the courage even amidst fear.

It was nice to spend a few weeks with Derrick and my mother before heading back to university. My mother thought she had lost me, she was not even sure in the first place, if I would be okay travelling on my own abroad. In her eyes, even if I was 19 years old, I was still a little child and she thought that this journey would still be a challenge for adults.

I had to go back to university even though, the wounds on my mouth had healed enough, and apart from losing some of my possessions from the bus, which probably had been stolen, I was feeling better and this "stuff", however precious it was, it was more important to be safe. It could have been worse, and my head was okay, I was just a little confused.

University continued, and soon I had to do my internship training. A friend of mine found me a place at NBS, a television company, I was in the marketing department, and I stayed with my two friends at Maker ere University during this time. It was closer and cheaper for us to share instead of me staying at my University which was further away.

Sarah and Tracy had been friends since we were 13 in Senior Bweranyangi school and we did almost everything together. We were there for each other throughout 'fall outs' with boyfriends, friends, parents, times when we did not have enough money, party time, "happy days", you name it.

As I had grown up without a television at home, I was not really into watching until my friends introduced me to a few series that I got so engrossed with.

One Sunday afternoon, Sarah's television had stopped working; we therefore all decided to go to watch from one of her friend's room, which was just two doors away in the same hostel. I was paying so much attention to the series that I almost did not see the rest of her visitors in the room, one of the visitors, Tom, later showed us a very funny video clip of young children who danced so well.

On my way, I wished that I had spent more time with Tom, but at the time, that was it. I did not turn back anyway.

A few weeks later, I had been left with the key to this same room to watch the series, as we had done before, the owner left to go and stay a night somewhere else. I watched the series and later put the key in the room we were staying in - as she had asked me to.

At around 11am while I was at work, I received a phone call to ask if I had removed Glenda's laptop and academic documents, I responded that I had not and would be there shortly to help her look for them.

We looked everywhere and I decided I would give her my own laptop that Danny and Annie had bought for me as it was same size with her, except hers was black and mine was pink. She would not listen, said she wanted her exact laptop. How on earth would I find it unless I found whoever had removed it, which seemed close to impossible? Later my friends and I realised that the point was not the laptop, she wanted her documents, and more so it was not finding who had taken the documents for she was already convinced that it was me who had stolen her documents. I cried, I did not know what to do I even thought about calling to ask Danny to pay for a new laptop, which would have been hard, as they had spent so much on me already and would not have been the solution that she wanted, which was her exact laptop and her documents. The time came, when we were supposed to both go and report the case to the police. I would have to write down a statement, the thought of which scared me, and as a suspect this meant I would probably have to spend a night in jail.

Fortunately, Glenda had spoken to her father who advised her to take me to her uncle who would decide how to handle this. We both went to Glenda's uncle who was working very close by. Glenda said all she had to say then I followed, as soon as I had finished speaking Glenda's uncle told her that "she is innocent" and did not see why she should even take me to police. He said, "why do you not even want to have Dora's laptop while we find a solution?" He also said that Glenda was lucky that I was offering it, and she would need it since she was doing an IT course. He added an example of somewhere close by there had been a robbery in an office, and despite the security cameras, more than fifty computers had been stolen; it was by then six months since the investigation with still no answers.

He advised her not to waste her time and money taking the case to police and more so to stop accusing an innocent person.

I was so relieved, went back to the hostel, and shared the news with my friends who had been waiting for me. I had to leave my internship place, as I had been away too long dealing with this. My friend Donah told me to apply at UBC, and this was great because I was given a place in the marketing department and it was also a television company.

As all this happened, I had no idea it was all about Tom, I had barely thought about him since we had met. I could not even recall much about him other than he was tall. Little did I know Tom had asked Glenda several times for my number, and because she liked him too, she had refused to give him my number. We later found out that she knew where her laptop and documents were but had just wanted to torture me because Tom apparently liked me.

When eventually, after Tom had told Glenda that "if luck would have it, we would meet again and she did not have to worry about giving him my number", she then decided to bring her phone to me saying, "here is someone who wants to speak to you". We spoke for such a long time and to her surprise, as I do not do this often, I had even given him my phone number.

Tom even asked to take me out as he had the sister's car and would like us to meet, however I declined this offer.

I started doing my training at UBC, we chatted on Facebook, sent text messages, had long phone calls, communicated several times a day and part of me longed to see him again as I could barely remember him.

I was in the saloon when I got a phone call from Tom saying he was in same town, and was out getting some popcorn for his sister Sky, who was pregnant and had been craving popcorn, I gave him directions to the saloon. He just passed and waved to me; that was it. We met at a friend's place later that evening, I did not speak much to him though, and my friend Sheila and Tom seemed to get on so well that they chatted till late. As soon as he had left, Sheila told me that Tom and I obviously liked each other, I dismissed it immediately, I told her it was my second time to meet up and I did not think I liked him anyway, other than as a friend.

We got on quite well, we got to know each other better, and Tom's friends kept asking him how he had suddenly got a very close friend who was a girl which was unusual.

On the other hand, my friends Pros and Daphne kept teasing me about Tom, Pros even joked and said, "if you don't accept him, I will snatch him, just because you like him". I still ignored this because to me, I thought we were good friends and I did not expect anything more, especially because I had just been in a relationship that had not worked out. I did not feel that I was ready for another relationship yet.

When I look back now, I can admit that yes, I liked Tom and maybe it was not easy to accept. I thought that if I was in a relationship, and it did not work out, then I would lose his friendship too.

Tom came to visit me at the hostel and with a few friends we would cook, play games and other times Tom would help to tidy up as we had our class discussions.

It was easier for Tom to visit as his university had been closed due to a strike so my friend Pross would tell me to use the chance "as I am not sure if he will have as much time when university re-opens".

We became so close, I felt very safe and happy being around Tom, I wanted to spend more and more time with him, and so we did. I was able to be myself, did not feel like I have to entertain him, or look fancy, we would chat play cards, or even have a nap when we got tired. He did not seem like a guest, or a new friend, it was as if I had always known him, having been close to my brother, it seemed like I had another brother, friend, not interested in relationships.

We stayed just friends until one evening when he was hugging me goodbye (in the same way he had done for a couple of months) we kissed. As soon as we had stopped, I became furious. I told him to leave my room and forget he had ever met me. I was so scared. I did not want to lose our friendship, but I was angry and sad because I felt that I should have seen this coming.

Tom tried to explain but I would not listen. I cried and sent him away. The following day, I went to the city shopping with my friend Pross, but Tom stayed on my mind, I had missed him so much, but still I did not want to call him. I knew that things would never be the same again, and thought if we started to have a relationship, and it did not work, I would have lost him. The following day, I called him and he said he had just been close to where I stayed but he did not know what my reaction would be if he arrived, so he had left.

He was at the time still on a motor cycle going back to his hostel. I asked him to turn around, and he did. Immediately he came through the corridor towards me, I jumped up and hugged him, we kissed and he carried me back to my room. I did not even care who was watching. I still think I was crazy, (if you have been to Uganda, you would realise that emotional displays are very different from what is ok in the UK). However, Tom carried me and then pecked me on my forehead and said, "let us let nature take its course". Tom also says that he will tell our children in future that the first time I kissed your mother, she cried!

I may also say that he cried too, when he was trying to explain and apologise?

It has been such a blessing to have Tom as a friend and boyfriend, I am glad we also had the time to know each other before dating.

Tom in his own words says:

> On the evening of Friday 30th September 2011 while I had gone to visit Doreen, She asked me, **"Tom can I trust you with my Heart"**. I looked her straight in the eye and responded with a **"YES"**.

That question and that response sealed a love so precious that has kept us together and never apart irrespective of the distance and out of physical contact situation.

I completed University, and stayed with friends Tracy and Pros so that we could split the rent. A few months before completing University, my mother had introduced me to Ben Male my late fathers friend, he was a great man, he had over twelve children staying in his mansion, he looked after them, would ring a bell for meal time, he would clean up after them, something unusual in Uganda, especially for a rich man. He was disabled, and had been the country's director of Sight Savers. He told me a lot about my father, and I looked up to his humble kind deeds. I still recall when he came to help me shift my stuff from the university hostel to a rental house after completing university. I could not believe it, not only did he offer to drive but also despite his disability, he helped to carry things from the hostel to the car. We were all moved, he also got on well with Tom, and they had a great chat especially about my late father.

Sadly, he slipped over in a tiled bathroom and died. I did not even get the chance to be at his funeral, but he was a man who worked and served others. I wish I had spent more time with him, but even the shortest time that we spent together will never be taken away from me; for he talked to me more from his kind deeds. Time indeed is the best gift anyone can offer for once you share your time with someone; you have given them part of your life that no one will ever take it away, not even death, nor fading memories.

CHAPTER FOUR

LEAVING UNIVERSITY

After I had finished, I missed University life, we had to move from house to house, look for jobs, pay rent, electricity, water and rubbish, sometimes the brokers would try to take advantage of us, and friends were always supportive, as we moved stuff from one house to another.

It was not easy waiting around to get jobs, I decided to use the money Danny and Annie had sent me to pay rent to start a mobile money business because it was said that there was a 100% guarantee that you would get the money back immediately after getting all the equipment. You could then decide what to do after that. It took several months, but I got through, went for the training and got all the equipment, however I had to withdraw the money from the line, instead of using it as capital, because I had to pay rent so the business was not able to take off.

We also started a restaurant at my former university, however we were robbed, everything was taken, even the used cooking oil. The rent had increased, and all the other working expenses, so unfortunately this business came to an end too.

Meanwhile, I learnt of a family friend who had one of the senior management positions at Mulago hospital. I went to her office, she was pleased to see me, she did not really remember me, as I was only young when she was last at home, but she knew my parents really well. She was excited to learn that I had undertaken a degree in entrepreneurship and business management. We had a discussion, and both thought it would be good for both of us if I worked managing personnel at her restaurant at UMA Lugogo, I started as soon as I could. Of course, my mother was over the moon, and told me that "it's a very good start and even if you are not given any pay, the experience is essential for your career and future". My friends and I were thrilled, how many students' complete university and get jobs almost immediately and more so in a management role? The answer was not many.

I was inducted to my job over the next few days, and went back to her home, where we had dinner together and talked about ways of improving the business. How to use proper marketing, or even perhaps using this beautiful space for wedding meetings, or other meeting etc. So far seemed so good, I could not wait to start working on it. I was fully involved in everything from piling up the bananas, book keeping to delivering the food. My attitude changed however when the director came one day and said, "by the way make sure you bank all the money from sales every day". I asked how, if I did that, would we have enough money for buying the shopping and paying workers? Her response was that she thought that the workers had been cheating her, so my job was now to investigate it. I did not agree, when she insisted I banked money, the first day I paid their wages from my own money. The following day I brought a few of my clothes to give one of the workers who had a daughter same size as me. The third day I went shopping to prove to her that they were not cheating her, and at this point the workers were so angry, they told me to do everything myself. I went shopping and I spent even more than they had spent, because not only did they buy from people who were giving them discount, but they also were strong enough to carry everything without needing to pay for transport. I carried a few things, but could not manage everything.

When I told the director the whole truth, she decided that I was now siding with them, I therefore knew that I would have to leave the job, unless she realised that there were other ways of boosting the business rather than blaming her workers; who had invested in so much energy and time that the last thing they could do was cheat a business that was not doing well.

It seemed like I was throwing away my only chance of a big job. I asked myself, did I need to be more patient, and was it too soon to quit a first job? Had I disappointed my mother, my friends, my guardians Annie and Danny? How could I go on with a job where workers were not paid after toiling and had young families?

Not long after that, I went for a job interview. It still sounds funny, the person interviewing me asked me, "were you ready for this interview? If your answer is yes, then you have just failed your interview, but if your answer is No, go home and I will let you know when you can redo your interview."

I responded a smart "No". I was therefore called a few days later, did my interview and started on my marketing job immediately.

Comparing the first job I had with this one, a few of my friends would laugh, "you surely, did not need to have gone to university to sell decoders on the streets" however there was a proper workplace where we all gathered, and the pay was good! I used the monthly pocket money to buy more decoders and resell, because our earnings were for commission only.

The most memorable thing about this job was that my friend Tracy and I decided to start using a saving box. Because at home we had often been without any spare coins - we would spend as much as we had, when we had it, without caring where the money for tomorrow would come from. At this time, I had also been talking to my mother and asking how everything was at home. This is when she told me that she could not get another loan, as she had not finished the salary loan she had taken out earlier to pay for my brother's tuition.

It was a coincidence that I had saved enough for my brother's tuition in my savings box so I immediately went to Ntinda town, which was near our residence, and deposited it into my mother's account. It was such a relief, as she was worried as it was the start of my brother's final year. I also bought my first set of chairs from my next savings.

Tracy and I visited Aunt Jessica, who gave us food, then we walked back home; she is a great cook. I met aunt Jessica during my first days at university, she had been at the opening bazar and was selling lots of delicious food. She kept looking at me from a distance, and when her niece mentioned that I looked like one of her daughters, she came up to me and told me so. This was a good surprise considering Faith was a few years younger than me, and from a completely different part of the country. I am from South West, and she is from the East and her dad from the North. We became close, it was like having a mum away from home, and as I write this, my biological mother and Jessica have met a few times now.

Life continued, one day travelling to work, I had been travelling with Almasi who had been to the same university with me, and had started restaurant when someone entered the taxi who had a very strong perfume on, the type that almost makes you stop breathing! As I got to my workplace, I jumped out of the taxi, looked back to wave to Almasi who was going further when suddenly I noticed a lady smiling at me in a mischievous way. I wondered why as I did not know her, apart from knowing that she had the strongest perfume I had ever come across. I got to the office, only to realise that my mobile phone was missing. I could not think of anyone else apart from the lady who had given me that smile, her face was still very clear to me.

I said to myself "it is only a phone let it go", it was also coming up to Christmas and soon I would be leaving the city and travelling back home. I would therefore not have enough time to look for her, and how would I even find her out of all the people in the city, who sometimes all look alike.

I was soon home, it was the first time in years as a grown up for all three of us; my mother, brother and I, to be home with our cousins to spend time together at Christmas. Of course, I went to check on my grandparents during this time but the evening chats with my mum were always great. Also, as a child, making her bed, I would sometimes play tricks on her by hiding her night dresses. I never outgrew this, would laugh as she looked for her night dress then later give it to her.

I was not home for long, I wished I could be, but because I had to go back to my job, I had to leave. However, compared to most people who were only supposed to be away for only Christmas day, I probably took a longer holiday than I should have done as I had stayed home until after New Year's Day, which of course my manager was not happy with. Ideally, because we were paid only commission, this should have been just up to the staff to choose.

A few days before heading back to the city for work, my uncle Manzi (elder brother to my late father) gave me some money to use as running capital for the mobile money business which I had not been able to start earlier as I had to use the money for rent.

On the 3rd of January I travelled back to Kampala (city). Just before we left my new mobile stopped working. My uncle and I just thought it was just a bad network connection, and it would be fine. Little did we know that the person who had stolen my original mobile phone the year before, had now used my phone to withdraw the money we had deposited on my mobile account number since I had not changed the pin. The pin number for the old phone of course, was as easy as A, B, C, so, she had managed to guess it!

When I arrived in Kampala, I stayed with my friend Pros, I could not understand why my phone card was not working. It started working the following day however, so I decided to go to a mobile money agent to withdraw the money from the account. I requested 400,000 shillings (which was less than what had been deposited on phone) but the agent said I did not have sufficient funds. I asked therefore for 5000, thinking this must be a joke and when he said that I still had insufficient funds on my phone, that is when it hit me that my money had been stolen. I immediately went to service centre to inquire for more information, and they told me the money had been withdrawn in Kampala (I had been travelling to Kampala at the time), but they would not help me find the person, as it would take a lot of time, and more money. They told me instead to take the case to police as they may know someone who knows about phone tracking.

I was a bit confused and angry with this lady, not only had she taken my phone, but almost a month later she had stolen my money.

Unfortunately, by the time I went back to the office, I found that the work meeting had started almost 10 minutes before I arrived. The manager said to me as I entered the door, "Doreen go back where you are coming from and do not return", so I left. He may have been joking, he did not give me any time to explain myself. However, I had also witnessed him do several things to the workers that I personally did not like. For example, once, one of my colleagues had sold to a customer who had not paid her and this boss had opened her bag, tossed everything from the bag, including toothbrush underwear all on the table in front of everyone at the office, saying there is not anything of value from your bag that I can even sell to get my money back. I did not like this, there were several other occasions like this, so this was a chance to leave. I later explained that he needed to treat people with respect, even when he was their boss. I am not sure if he ever changed, but I was quite surprised that he gave me a good reference for the next stage of my journey: volunteering on Iona.

Not forgetting the lady, who had stolen my phone, I decided to track her down - not just for my phone and the money, but because I thought she may also do it to someone else. I wrote a statement at Wandegeya police station, I had said that I would recall who she was if I could see her again and smell her perfume, and a few weeks afterwards the policeman called the number of the person who had my phone, she said she was in town selling food, he told her that he would come to buy some food. He asked me to go along with him, but I declined as I knew she may most likely recognise me. I stayed at the police station, no sooner had she entered the building, then I smelt her perfume; she had my phone of course, no doubt as it matched everything from the blue colour, to the serial number.

She denied having stolen it and when I asked if she recognised me she responded, "no I look like my mother, maybe it is her you have seen her before!!" It was a strange response, but yes, she did look like her mother.

I was leaving the country in the next few weeks for Scotland, so I left it at that. It seemed as if I would not have time; they kept postponing the meetings, and she claimed she that she had got the phone from her brother who works as a conductor in a taxi, and was upcountry, and may not be back to the city for months.

Two years later I discovered that the policeman who had worked on my case had been transferred to my village, what a coincidence? However, it was sad to "out" the lady because her mother, and a few of her friends, died after a mob carried out their own justice, when people realised that stealing had been their family business for years. I wished better justice had happened, but it was too late.

Tracy and I had called this phone of mine, "blueberry", not exactly a smart phone, but we both liked it, and I left it with her as I travelled to Scotland.

January 2013, was when I finally graduated, Annie and Danny travelled to Uganda for my graduation, we visited some of their old friends, visited my family and my grandmother who was thrilled when they greeted her in my local language. During their stay, Danny asked me how old my grandmother was, to which I immediately looked at her and asked how old she was, she said I am not certain, but I think I am 10 years old, we laughed so much, because some of her great grandchildren are more than 12 least. She was joking, but she could have been serious as there had been little or no birth records during the time she grew up.

The good thing about not having a job, was that I could spend enough time with my friends and my other family Annie and Danny who took me to took Lake Mburo National Park, Murchison falls, which was splendid.

At the day of my graduation, Tom had been travelling back from Fort Portal, it was a nice day, but finally when he arrived and Danny could not resist saying that there was "brightness in my face". We took several pictures, and Tom kept saying "get closer to me" at which point my mother knew that he was my boyfriend.

I will never forget my mother's face when they brought her mushroom soup. The graduation lunch was a present from Annie and Danny which was paid for by Annie. It was therefore at one of the 5 star hotels in Uganda; Serena. My mother, was not used to soup, and expected much more from such a big hotel. Her face said it all when they put it on the table; "is that all?"

This was not the first time my mother had met Tom, she had met him earlier when I had malaria and she had come to help. Pros (who was also unwell) and I had been craving bread and my mother could not leave the house alone to get the bread. Most of my friends who came to visit were bringing splash, other good things, but not bread which is what I wanted most.

That evening Tom brought me bread, my mum and I were happy about this, and she kept mentioning how he was "a true friend who knew exactly what I wanted". I later discovered that Tom had brought bread because it was one of the cheapest things that he knew that I liked, and would possibly manage to eat even when I was not feeling well.

When my mother kept talking about Tom, I thought she must have figured that he was my boyfriend so I waited for her to ask me more but she never did.

It was a great graduation, normally two guest cards would be given to enter the university square, so my two mums both attended, whereas my dad listened from close by. My mother gave me a goat as a graduation present, during the party just after she had said made her speech, John called from home to say the goat had delivered two kids, making them 3 in total. Both my mum's, dad, Tom, and I attended two more parties. I then shared a house with Tracy and Pros, and we stayed together in Uganda for at least a month.

CHAPTER FIVE

VOLUNTEERING ON IONA

It was sad to say goodbye to Annie and Danny they had become part of our small family; however, Danny advised me to consider applying for voluntary work on Iona, it would cost a lot to pay for tickets and visas but he said he would pay for all these if I wanted to go.

He thought that this would be good for my CV, experience and would definitely be better than staying without a job. I applied, I did not get a placement the first time I asked. I was told that it was not easy to get a visa from Africa and it would cost the Iona Community money, for sponsorship etc. However, when Danny explained to them that he would be sponsoring my tickets and visa and I had visited the UK before as their guest, which meant that I had a greater chance of getting a visa. Later I got a letter to say I had been accepted as a volunteer on Iona beginning on 15th May 2013 which I accepted.

Danny and Annie helped me with the necessary requirements to travel; they picked me from the airport then took me to Iona the night before my start date. We stayed at the hostel, the route to the hostel was so long. It was cold and very windy, I did not like it; wondered how I would suffer the next few months in this cold climate?

We all shared a room at the hostel, had a lovely meal and the following day headed to Iona Abbey to start as a volunteer, we were warmly welcomed by Karen who was the staffing co coordinator at that time. There was then an induction session, and we were shown our accommodation; Cul-Shuna, was such a beautiful place by the sea. I could see the sea from my bed, and could clearly hear the waves.

One of the experiences I had as a volunteer was to to see someone who was blind for the first time. We all knew there was going to be a blind guest, so we needed to make sure there is enough room for entry and exit, for fire escape reasons. Later during the meal, I was looking around to see who it was but could not work it out. For some reason, I had imagined that this person would be eating on their own. A few minutes later however, I saw someone across the table, trying to put food on his fork but missing it each time. I suddenly knew that he was the one, I felt very emotional, and was crying. He was just opposite me, and spoke and acted like everyone else, until he missed the food. The thought of him not being able to see, and not knowing what the colour of the food was, made me cry. However, when someone else came who was blind, together with his family of two young boys of about 4 and 6 years, and their mother, I began to learn more. Each week we show the guests how to do their chores, and this week, during the first session, the blind man's son put his hand up and said, "I have a question: What do you do if you are a child and the adult who is meant to help you carry a big tray is blind?" We were all touched by how this young child, and his siblings, had matured and were always running to help their father. I have learned so much from all these experiences.

I had a great experience and decided to apply for a visa extension to volunteer longer. Unfortunately, my passport was sent back to the wrong address: two doors next to where I was staying. I waited in vain and later went to stay with Annie and Danny to wait for news about my visa. It passed the deadline for notification; I could not leave the country without a passport no longer could I stay without a visa.

We contacted the Immigration Office, and found out that because the neighbours did not know the owner of the package, and it was marked "confidential", they had decided to forward it back to the main visa office who never contacted us. However, we were told that I could stay until I had got my passport. Thankfully, I had been granted the visa.

I went back to Iona as soon as I could, and I also applied for one of the staff jobs. My dad Danny bought me a new suit and shoes for my big interview. However, I twisted my ankle at the ceilidh the night before the interview so actually did not manage to put on the shoes! Danny came over and stayed on Iona, we had conversations, and we spoke about the questions (and answers) of what we thought I might be asked at the interview. It turned out to be the best interview I have ever had, not only because I got the job, but because I felt comfortable enough to be myself.

When I was asked what my fears would be, and said, "being homesick, cold and scared of staying in a big room on my own". The Centre Director promised she would give me a teddy bear to keep me company which we all thought it was so funny.

The Cul-Shuna family could not wait to know about the news of the job, which of course I shared as soon as I could. They had all been supportive, driven me to my interview venue, brought me food, given me ideas of how to approach questions and kept me in their prayers.

CHAPTER SIX

A RESIDENTIAL STAFF JOB ON IONA

I got the job to work as a housekeeper in the resident team from 2014. I was therefore, before the job started, able to go to back to Uganda, spend some time with Tom, friends and family before returning to Iona in February 2014 for the staff training. This time with my mother was very special, especially because I was a grown up, and we could discuss issues at her workplace, my future, our family in general.

I applied for the visa to return to the UK, and within a few working days I had been granted it. This was not an easy decision, I was worried about leaving my grandmother who was by then old, and I did not know how it would be, spending almost a year without seeing Tom. However, Tom encouraged me.

He told me that it would make more sense if at least one of us had a job, we then had a better chance of starting a family. He told me he would communicate as much as he could. It was not going to be easy, but he said it would be good for my career too. We also hoped that he could apply to come and volunteer on Iona or at least to visit.

It was very sad to say goodbye, but I could not have been more proud of Tom. He supported me in the decision, and was there to encourage me, even when sometimes I thought I should just give up and stay home with him. It just shows me how selfless he is.

Most things were very new and different, yet in some ways a lot seemed the same. I had a great season, I arrived a few days before the training, in February. I must say, that although I enjoyed seeing snow in real life, other than on the television and post cards, I did not like the cold weather. It was colder than I had anticipated, especially in the Abbey and the pilgrimage training was held on a very cold and rainy day. However, meeting new people, having enough time to get to know each other by having informal social meetings, telling our stories and sharing meals at the house I stayed in, was the best part of the training; especially because the fire was lit! There were times when I had to wear up to twelve layers of clothes to keep warm. I could not believe that other people just wore two layers, or even less.

As part of the staff training and team building, we organised to go to Camas which is an outdoor centre for the Iona Community based on Mull. We were there for a day, we played team building games, had a meal together and were given a very good example of what living and working in a community meant, which has been very helpful to me.

We were asked to look around the room, looking for red, then we would shout out anything that is red, then we were asked to look for green and we would shout out what is green. Later, they explained to us that when you are looking for a certain colour, you will easily see it. It will be more visible and the rest will be less visible. Just like with people, everyone has something good in them, and if we look for the good in people we will find it.

I led a service in the Abbey Church about this, and encouraged people to look for the good in themselves, others and situations. This training has also helped me in the management role for volunteers; I encourage them to do what they enjoy and are good at. Often when new people arrive, I try and look for their strengths, and this helps the whole team. People are always good at something. It has helped me to live in a big shared accommodation.

The best part of working in the hospitality team is the fun we have together. The tea breaks, the laughter while hanging laundry, chatting with guests during task team training. The slogan is "if you make a mistake, it does not matter; it can be fixed". One of my favourite memories is Zekka, who had such a great sense of humour. I had found her using a mop head that we do not usually use in the kitchen, I told her, "you are using the wrong mop head. I will forgive you today, and the second time, but you do not want to know what will happen the third time". After a few days, I found her again using the wrong mop head, when I asked her what had happened, she said, "you said you would forgive me the second time and this is the second time". I laughed so much, but never worked out whether she did this on purpose, or if it was an accident. She still made my day anyway, and every time we meet we still laugh about it

It was a great year, lots of memories, lots of fun. It was easy to play tricks on people, joke, and still get on well. I remember the day I went around offering different people an empty banana. Over 85% of the people accepted, and occasionally someone would ask I wonder why Dora is offering me an empty banana skin, and say "are you sure it is a banana", then I would laugh.

Not after long after this joke, it was my birthday and Sarah, who was a very good friend, and my line manager at the time, organised a delicious banana cake in the shape of ketchup bottle on top for my birthday.

The time came to blow out the candles, this was at the meal with all the guests. I tried so many times to blow out the candles, but every time I thought I had done it, they would relight. When I had almost run out of breath, and of course not worked out why the candles would not go out, Robin came and saved me. When she had taken the candles away, Sarah told me that it was their chance to play a trick on me. She was getting her own back and had therefore put magic candles on the cake. I had never seen, or heard of them before, so I had no idea. She therefore won.

CHAPTER SEVEN

A FIRST CHRISTMAS ON IONA

Christmas was a glorious day. A few people even went swimming. There were very few guests, and these guests really wanted to be on Iona, so it made a great difference. The house party felt like a big family. I had never had a Christmas sock before, we had made candles, crafts all together and at breakfast Santa brought presents for everyone, staff and guests. This made it even more special, all of us relaxed eating and spending time together.

A few weeks before Christmas, there had been some misunderstandings amongst the staff, and even a few people had left. However, kindness, care and love stayed and remained to shine through everyone. I had been checking my emails, which I do not do very often. Staff are allowed a few days each year to have friends or family to come and visit and to stay overnight at their accommodation. However due to shared space and other reasons, one has to email a request to the staffing coordinator and also inform the rest of the people sharing the accommodation. I therefore sent an email to all the staff, apologising first for sending the request so late, and secondly letting them know that a friend of mine would be visiting over Christmas. No one needed to worry about where he would stay, I went on to say, for whoever opened their door when he knocked, he would be happy to share with them. It went on, and on, and at the end I said, "his name is Jesus".

When people started to read of my guest they probably wondered why I had not let them know of this in advance, as soon as they read his name; they laughed and said it was so nice. Considering the email came at the time when most staff were struggling, I loved their responses and how everyone worked together.

Most people responded to it with the relevance to their job. For example, the Sacristan asked, "if he would be coming as an adult or child, to know if he would save him wine, or fruit juice, for communion". The Cook asked, "if he had any special dietary requirements", the Musician, asked, "if he played any instruments", the Housekeeper asked me to remind him that "for safety and hygiene reasons he could not come to the kitchen in sandals", the Shop Manager told me to "tell him about late night shopping and offers of hot chocolate".

Almost every single staff member responded and when I asked who would be picking him up at the jetty, (ferries - weather dependant), before the maintenance staff could respond. Sharon who was the deputy director responded that, "we needed not to worry about ferries as Jesus could walk on the water".

I enjoyed all their responses and had no idea when I wrote the email, that it would turn out like this. This was also very good however, as it was a learning curve too, to see how many people you "have to" speak to, just to have a friend visit. I realised that this sometimes affects the actual act of hospitality.

The New Year was full of hope and energy, the night started in the village hall, with lots of games, families dancing, and most of the people from the island were all packed in the village hall.

We played a board game, "qwirkle" which I found at our accommodation. I also had a lovely chat with Tom. He had sent me some nice flowers on WhatsApp!

Distance may keep us apart, but the bond of love between us will always bring us close.

We had a delicious breakfast at the Abbey flat; Shalome invited Richard, Marcus and me to take blessings for the New Year. Later together with most of the staff, we went for a walk to a lovely sandy bench Port Ban, and Shalome waited for us in the community's green van where she celebrated communion with us. It was a special way to begin a new year.

CHAPTER EIGHT

ACCESSIBLE TOILETS FOR UGANDA

Having grown up in a school for children with disabilities, it was always heart-breaking to see children of my age, and even younger, crawling on dirty floors to use the pit latrines, which are just a hole in the ground. I occasionally would clean the latrines, but because we all shared same latrines and there were many of us, they were dirty most of the time; and I did not know how to clean them well enough either. I knew from when I was aged about 7 years that I wanted to make sure the children with disabilities had better facilities, and hoped that someday in the future, when I was a grown up, I could do something to make this come true.

During my second season on Iona, having learnt about the accessible toilets in the UK, and even sneaked into the public accessible toilets to see how different they were, I started talking to some of my friends and colleagues. They advised me to start raising money and to spread the awareness about the need for accessible toilets in Uganda.

Amazingly, different people came up with different ideas. The first one was Elizabeth who was a volunteer and carried out a "haggis drive" game. It was fun and people donated money. A quiz followed, again donations given.

Sharon also spoke to her Iona family group the Ross of Mull and Iona, who I then did a presentation for, and they supported the project.

Georgina was a young girl from Glasgow, who loved her hair, also took up the challenge saying: "we shall not offer to God offerings that cost us nothing". She cut several inches off her hair, and donated it to the Princess Trust, which is a charity that support children with cancer. Lots of people sponsored her to cut her hair, and she donated the money raised to the Ugandan toilet Project.

Joyce Watson, who is one of the residents living who has lived the longest on the island of Iona, decided that the challenge for her 70th birthday was to climb one of the Ben Lowers. She did this with her cousin and a friend, and said it was not easy, but thinking of the need for accessible toilets in Uganda gave her the reason and courage to continue climbing.

A few weeks after that, word about the project had spread, a friend of mine called Angela who is an associate of the Iona Community told me she had dreamt of reading an article about me, and the project in the Coracle (which is the quarterly magazine of the Iona Community) we laughed about it, then I also said some dreams do come true so I ought to find out more about this magazine. Angela and I did more research about the Coracle, got in touch with Neil who is the editor, he said yes, so a few friends helped me to write an article and it was then published. Following this, other members of the Iona Community found out about the project, and through the Iona family groups, and individuals, continued to support this cause.

I was also invited to deliver a short session about the project during the summer Iona Community members "community week". The theme for this week was about "becoming change makers", this meant that even more community members donated money, and we had also gathered a team together who had different ideas for the project

There were very many different other ways of raising funds, Shalome, the shop manager, also a hairdresser, cut people's hair and donated the money raised, we had a ceilidh at the village hall with teas, coffee and a cake made by Anja the Abbey cook. I was invited to speak at different churches, also different people talked to their home churches about the project and some of them, for their annual charitable giving, donated money for the toilet project.

Cara, who is an Iona Community member, took the idea of having a donation box outside the welcome centre toilets to help support this project. When the Iona Council agreed, Richard who is my friend and colleague, suggested that it might be amusing if there could be an actual toilet in which to collect the money for the toilet project. It started as a joke. Later when I told Shuggie who is a local, and long term maintenance team staff member, said that actually he did have a real toilet that was no longer required. Therefore, he adapted it to enable people to put money into. This toilet box has now been outside the welcome centre for over a year, and we have got a lot of donations through it.

Caitlin, a former staff member also helped me create a "go fund me" webpage which is an online giving page, and through this, lots of money has also been raised.

By the time I went back home to Uganda at the end of the season, we had enough money to construct a set of 4 toilets, two changing rooms, a 500 litre water tank, solar power, buy cleaning equipment, pay someone to help clean and show children how to use these facilities, in two different schools. The first was to be constructed at Tukore Primary School. This is where I went to school when I was young and where my mother teaches sign language. My late father was also one of the founders of this school. Later, we planned to undertake the same design and construction for another school called Ishekye Integrated School.

One of the first challenges I faced a few months after I had started the fundraising, came when I phoned home, having told my mother about the project earlier and asked my brother Derrick to take a few pictures of the school, and the pit latrines, so that the people who I was meeting could understand what exactly I was talking about.

When Derrick started taking the pictures however, the Director of the school called him in and said he did not approve of this. This was because there were a lot of disagreements going on at that time, and there was a rumour that my brother wanted to take over the school, despite him saying clearly that he had no intentions of this sort.

My brother was understandably very upset, and decided to delete the pictures. He told me to stop raising the money as he felt that the people I was trying to help were not grateful enough. I knew this was because he was upset, and I told him that I was doing it for children with disabilities, therefore I would continue with the project, even if it meant starting with another school for children with disabilities.

I just wanted to make sure children with disabilities had better facilities no matter where they were from. It would have been good to start with the school we had both gone to, but it would not stop me from helping other schools. It all calmed down though, when the Director of the school and the rest of the local community realised that I was only trying to support the school, and that my brother was not trying to take over control. They then allocated us the place to do the construction.

When I got back to Uganda we bought the cleaning equipment. I went shopping with my cousin Mercy, and so many people did not know much about the coloured mopping buckets. Several people in town kept asking us if they were for sale and what they were for. We had got them from the biggest supermarket in my home town; they would normally only be used in big offices or rich homesteads.

I first saw them on Iona, but had not realised how unusual they were. When the children saw the mops, they were very appreciative. They could not believe that mopping could happen without having to bend down. They danced while trying to demonstrate to me how nice it was to have these long mops; much better than using old rags and a basin where you have to bend over to do the cleaning, which is always hard for children with disabilities.

I had already signed a contract to return to Iona, but recognised that this could always change due to unpredictable circumstances, or if I was not granted the visa. So, Sarah and Ali organised a farewell party for me, just in case I did not return. My favourite dishes were served: chicken, banana bread, and of course ketchup all on the menu, and there was lots of singing and games. We played musical chairs, pass the parcel and many other games. It was a great evening.

The staff also gave me presents of two Iona T-shirts which Tom and I both wore when I got home. Tom's mum thought this was hilarious (we looked like twins). I was also given a portable solar power bank, this was rather very thoughtful as I was going back to Tukore and my family roots, a village where there is no electricity so it was handy to have a solar charger.

On my way home, Georgina, her mother, Angela, my dad Danny and mum Annie, plus Sharon, Jen, Sarah surprised me by appearing at the airport. I was pleased, even more pleased that they did the Mexican wave, which is the traditional Iona wave at the jetty when people are leaving - it had suddenly become rather international.

Tom, Tracy and James met me at the airport when I returned home; it was lovely to see them again.

I stayed in Kampala where I met up with a few of my friends, and also visited Tom's sisters home where we celebrated my 25th birthday. Tom and I planned to visit his parents, and then later go on to visit my mother. This was going to be the first time I would meet them I was therefore nervous, however I felt at home as soon as I got there, I could even help with cooking, washing up and Toms mum dad sisters were all lovely. Tom's mum told me stories of when he was young; he was rather embarrassed!

I taught the small children a few songs. We went shopping, walking, and visited the Toro palace, I loved Fort Portal, it is a beautiful part of the country. By the end of my stay I was already feeling as part of the family, on the first night Tom's sister Mattie gave me a glass of milk and coffee beans and said traditionally it is a sign of welcome to the family. Tom's dad said I was welcome back anytime. Surprisingly, we did not manage to leave that day, so had to come back even after I had said my goodbyes.

I was meeting up with the toilet project engineer though so the following day Tom and I travelled to my home, his mother had packed gifts for my mother and this meant so much. She even gave me a length of cloth and a goat, she also has a great sense of humour so we got on well.

We had a good time at my home too, my aunt Dorcas, mother, brother and cousin Mercy were all there. My mother was very nervous, it was almost like she was going to meet her father-in-law, I now understand it. It was very different from the first time when she had met Tom, knowing he was only my friend, he was now a future son in law so she behaved differently.

Tom stayed the night, I took him around our village, then he left the following day. I started finding out more information about the location of the accessible toilets at the school which seemed to take forever. I was now wondering if there would be enough time, especially because of the upcoming presidential elections, and having to apply for my visa. I did not want anything to get in my way. I wanted by the time I left the country to come back to the UK, for the toilets to be done and did not want to have to rush.

It was a good thing the Board of Directors and a representative of the Teachers and Parents Association had showed my mother the place where we should construct the toilets. We soon started to build, but half way through the project, the engineer was involved in an accident. The work did not stop however since all the other workers were there, but it delayed a bit.

I learned a lot from supervising this project, for example, that the times when it rained heavily, soil could not be transported on truck. It was nice to go to the site bringing a few sugar canes and chatting with the builders and constructors; they were great people who worked so hard and were not sure of where next job will come from.

When we went to the next school to do the construction, this school even had some blind students, they all were very appreciative. I remember one of the Head Teachers bursting into tears, saying

"God must have sent you to provide toilets, as the students here really need them". She explained that most parents could not, or would not pay school fees for disabled children, so even when they had piped water, they could not afford to have flushing toilets.

At this school, the water supply had been cut off; I had to go to National Water and Sewage Corporation to pay for water so that we could get the water needed for construction. The well was a long way away, and this was a problem for the children with disabilities. Even for able bodied people it is tiresome to carry water so far.

We shopped again for the mops and buckets, children were happy to use the long mops, they thought it was quite fun to mop while standing. It was moving to see how much they appreciated and were pleased at every small detail; like, toilet roll holders.

When I got back to the UK I got an opportunity to visit Sharon, who was a friend of my late father. She lives in Suffolk, my mother had always wanted me to visit, but organising holidays, and the expense of that, was not as easy as she had imagined.

One of the staff however was training in London, and she helped me go through London, and invited me to spend a night at her sister's home.

Sharon met me on the train, her two sons, that I had known from when we were little, had also taken time off work to meet up. It was a good reunion. I know we played together as children, but do not know what language we used, as my brother and I did not know much English then except... "how are you?" and "I am fine". Most children in Uganda know this.

I was warmly welcomed, and as Sharon prepared dinner, I went through lots of old pictures of her time in Uganda, several from them from my father's school.

Later, Sharon put on a video. I watched the video, particularly looking at the details of disabilities and wheel chairs, a few moments on, I wondered why the person in the video seemed familiar. He looked a bit like my brother, but my brother was not disabled, later it hit me that this was my late father. It was bitter sweet, emotional sight, yet I was glad I had seen it; I recorded it with my phone. We only had a few pictures of my father, usually in black and white, but seeing a video seemed almost like I had seen him in person. It was heart breaking to see how he tried to walk, the weakness in his bones, I had no idea how serious it was until then.

In the background, Sharon talked about how my father was disabled himself, but did his best to help and support others who were disabled. This motivated me, and encouraged me to continue doing whatever I possibly could to help people with disabilities.

It was sad, but nice to see the video, where school pupils sang a song we all used to sing very often during morning parade when I was at the school. When we sang it, we used to sing it to the late Dan Basiime, it was good to see in the video, pupils addressing and singing to my father in person. Seeing him seated in front of the choir, something I would never have known if it was not for this video, made me feel emotional. I still have the video clips on my phone and know the chorus by heart.

> The window of Joy is sitting over Tukore
> The window of Joy by Dan Basiime
> Transformation in this area
> Tukore is now sailing on again.

The time spent with Sharon felt very precious; she took me out to her garden, also to visit a school in her town for children with disabilities where she is an Occupational Therapist.

We had long conversations. She even told me lots of things about my father that I had never heard before. I had always wanted to speak to my mother about my father, but I worried she would get upset, so we had never spoken much about him. But now I feel more comfortable, and we have spoken about him more in the last 2 years, than we ever did in the years before.

I was sad to learn that my father's death could have been prevented by antibiotics, but it was too late. Sharon told me that because, HIV was new in the country, and there was a lot of discrimination, and rumours that everyone who was not well, was dying of AIDS, my father did not want to go to the hospital, and only went much later, when Sharon insisted. She told him that even if everyone was saying he was HIV positive, it was important to find out the truth. When the results came back, they were negative. He did not have HIV, but instead had brucellosis, caused by drinking unpasteurised milk, which could have been prevented or treated, but it was by then too late, so he died.

I also remember in primary school an occasion where a man, who was working at my school, called me and asked me if I "was a daughter to Dan Basiime", when I said yes, he said "ooh your father died of AIDS". I think I must have asked my mother who then told me that "when you grow up you will find out about him dying, but for now you should know he did not die of AIDS and that I love you" which is very important.

However, I am glad, I feel at least I got a second chance to see my father. I also planned to show the film to my brother when I returned home, however I could not work out when the right moment would be to do that. In fact, he later saw the film when I was showing him some other film and photo's. He was very excited, printed out the pictures and took some to his house, my mother's house, my grandmother's house and could not believe that I had not showed him before. My mother and I were very touched by his reaction. It was very significant to me, as it was the first time my brother, mother and I were able to talk openly about my late father.

It was the start of healing; I thanked my mother physically for all she has done for us. My mother even said, "you are now old enough that I could remarry", she may have been joking, but it was the first I ever heard her say this with a happy spirit. I am so blessed to have my mother in my life, even if I was given the choice of who to choose to be my mother, I would still choose my mum.

I also showed the video of my father to his brother, my uncle told me that he thought my father and I had much in common, even if I had not met him. He told me that my father would have also helped people, he was kind and my uncle thought that he had passed this on to me.

It was very touching to hear these words from him; he is a very gentle and loving man, my closest uncle whose wife is also my godmother. They are hospitable and usually have a full house and provide food to so many people in the village. My uncle also has a daughter, who is wonderful, everyone at home and whoever meets her loves her, she loves people too.

My cousin, suffered from cerebral malaria when she was very young, fortunately she survived, and though she can do almost every domestic chore, sing happily, there are things that she does not understand. She would often ask her mother and my uncle to find her a husband, kept questioning why other sisters were getting married, but no one was finding her a husband. She loves babies so much, and often would ask to cuddle them in church and look after them. Unfortunately, a man who should be respectable, and was old enough to be my father, took advantage of this innocent girl. I used to think, I could easily forgive, but it was so hard for me to forgive after this. I was so full of anger and disappointment. I had grown up with her, we had learnt how to peel bananas together, we would sweep the compound together, we would cook when the adults were out in the garden. She was my elder, yet sometimes younger sister, and I love her so much and she is always a friend.

No one knew what she was going through, they thought she had just put on weight and by the time they realised it was too late, she was already 6 months pregnant. My cousins mother who is also my Godmother, found it very difficult and as a family we all did, it was tough to forgive the man who did this. However, my Godmother later said, all in all it is good, a child is a blessing and her daughter always wanted a child and maybe no one would have asked for her hand in marriage. Her forgiving and unique behaviour was unbelievable. I am now a Godmother to my cousin's lovely son, and hope to look after him like my own, with love and care; he is a blessing to the whole family. Through him we have seen love, forgiveness, understanding, challenges that we have learnt from as individuals and a family.

With some of the savings from my Iona pay, my uncle helped me secure a small piece of land in our home town, I also managed to contribute towards my cousin's school fees and my mother's house construction.

Education is very important, I wish every child could go to school, I have been fortunate enough to go to school but a big percentage of the population in Uganda do not get the chance to have a higher education. There are a lot of children who drop out of school. My aunt, younger sister to my mother, did not go to higher classes due to lack of school fees. She used to look after us, and my grandmother, when we were little.

During her visits to my mother's school, my aunt fell in love with Tayebwa, who was a deaf student at my mother's school at the time. They later got married and now have five wonderful children who are very smart but are always worried about tuition. My aunt is a peasant, and her husband trained as a carpenter, so gets some money, but not enough for a big family.

It is fortunate that I have been able to pay for their school fees, but I'm not sure yet if I will be able to afford their University studies. Their children are intelligent and their parents are wonderful too, I hope the children can get a good education that their parents were not able to.

Joyce McIntyre is a nurse on Mull and lives on Iona running a taxi and bed and breakfast business with her husband. I first met her at the GP surgery. She told me that she had spoken to a few of the guests who stayed at her bed and breakfast about the Ugandan toilet project, and they had donated money, which she gave to me. I did not even know her at this point, but was touched by this. She invited me for a meal a few months later and told me that she was going on a medical trip with her friend to Uganda. We chatted more about Uganda so that she could have an idea what to except.

Whilst I was back in Uganda at the end of the season, Joyce visited and we met up for a meal, she even had a package for my mum from my Iona friends and a photo album for most memories of twenty one months on Iona.

Joyce and her friend also managed to fit in her tight schedule time to come and visit my mother's school, they brought a football and lots of clothes in a suitcase, and a suitcase full of medication for the school. They also got to see the accessible toilets which were at the time still under construction.

Both my mother and I were thrilled, at being able to have friends from Iona visiting. They even spent a night at my mother's house, it was very, very, special. This was a time well spent reconnecting with everything and everyone.

It was hard to believe when the time came to go back to Iona that I was leaving home again already; time flew so quickly. It was even harder this time to say goodbye to Tom. There were times I said and wished, "can't I just stay at home?", but Tom was always supportive. He told me that we would not be apart forever, it was just a matter of time.

We have been lucky to have friends who have taken things to Tom and my mother from Scotland, and brought stuff back for me. It means so much. Every little connection is important when the person you love is miles away. I always buy same shower gels and sprays, lotions as Tom, so that we will be using the same ones. It may not seem very much, but it makes me happy to know that Tom is wearing same deodorant as me, even from miles away. It has not been easy however, but has made us stronger and built our trust.

I returned mid-April for my third season as a resident on Iona. So much seems the same on Iona this year, yet a lot seems different at the same time.

CHAPTER NINE

A THIRD SEASON ON IONA

No single day on Iona is actually the same, yet the routine is what keeps the place running. Even at mealtimes, the same words that have been used for many years end the meal such as: "is anyone eating with us for the first time?" "Is anyone leaving us before the next meal", or sometimes the person chairing the meal adds, "knowingly for the last time", where people always burst into laughter.

Iona is a very special place, but we all know it is the people who make the place even more special. It amuses me how wonderful people are; I have learned so much being on Iona. Sometimes you think, "well I have been here for a few years now", however every single day is a new opportunity for learning. With different tourists, new staff, new guests every week, there is so much to learn and hold onto.

This year I have worked with one of the most amazing people I have ever met (to date of course) and one amongst many. It was not always easy, but a learning curve. As soon as the first group of volunteers arrived, I learnt that one of them had Asperger's syndrome, I did not know much about what it meant, but he was amazing. He told me everything I needed to know about his experience of living with the condition. One day when we were both working, he told me how he liked things done in a certain way, and that routine and order were very important to him, which he explained was because of his condition. I understood this, and made sure he always had proper instructions, I also told him to ask me as many questions as he needed to, whenever he did not understand something. Later, he upset other volunteers who could not understand why he always acted like this; wondered why he always wanted things done his way. He would also change round things if they were not done quite in the way he wanted. I understood him, understood them, but did not know how to make sure they understand and get on with each other.

I tried to explain to the other volunteers, I also tried to explain to him. I used examples that I thought would be quite simple to understand, I said "when you are walking in a group like we do on a pilgrimage, some people are used to walking very fast, others not as fast, but when it is supposed to be a walk for the whole group, both parties must "make an effort" to get to a compromise so that they are not too slow or too fast!"

I also gave an example; "because we are a team, sometimes someone else may set the beakers in different colours when you would prefer them to match". I continued to say, "when this is done, do not change them, but when you are the one setting the table, next time, you can match them as you would like. For teamwork to happen, there has to be compromise, we have to sometimes let people do what they like, even when it is not what we would prefer".

I was not sure whether any of this would actually work, but surprisingly it did and by the end of their time together, we had built a team. It was not that they started liking what the others were doing, but there was a higher level of acceptance and compromise.

The biggest learning curve for me and the other volunteers came, when it was time to say goodbye to the volunteer with Asperger's syndrome. He told us how we had given him a chance to work with us, despite the differences and difficulties he felt that he had caused. He said that he had not often had opportunities to do this, and this had been the best part of his life.

I looked at this volunteer and as he continued to speak, we were both touched and in tears. His words were so moving and though it had been difficult, all of us had learned so much from him, and he had also learned a lot from us.

As I write this, I have only been away from home for six months, but so many things have already happened. The challenges have made me stronger and I have had moments when I have felt "so alive".

A short time after arriving on Iona for this season, my only brother Derrick was hit by a car; it was one of the hardest times of being away from home. I called my mother several times, but sometimes I could almost hear her trembling on the phone. I felt so sad, that I could not be there for my brother and my mother who most needed me at this time. What made it even harder was that the doctors were worried that the head injury may have damaged his brain. This, I knew, could mean anything. Part of me was very happy that he had survived. I tried so hard to keep that in my mind, because my greatest fear was returning home and realising that the person I grew up with, had lost all his memory and could not even remember who I was.

Amidst all of this, I still had to be present and active at my workplace. There were new volunteers that needed training, new guests arriving every week, and almost nothing stops on Iona. You also still have to get on with, and develop relationships with, the other staff. This is not always easy. I could not have gone through it on my own, but the lovely, caring and supportive people who have not just been colleagues, but family away from family, helped me to get through this.

People supported me in different ways; messages, cards, flowers, parents, medical bills, giving me hugs and checking for updates. Even when no one had met my family, I did not feel like I was facing this on my own.

At the same time my neighbour at home had lost her child who was 8 years old. He had learning disabilities, and had been such a close friend of mine. I loved Quinton, he would run to me all the time, ride on my back, I would take him around the playground, anywhere, sometimes people, even his mother, would say "he will pee on you or even worse, so you need to put him down", but I never did.

I feel sad that he will not be at home when I next return, and that I was not there during his last days. He showed me how to love, smile, play, be young at heart. I loved his innocence, beauty, I am glad I shared some time with him. All I have left of him are several pictures on my phone but the memories will last forever.

On July 19th, my brother's wife gave birth to a baby boy. It was time to celebrate, my mother is now a proud grandmother, this was a few weeks after my brother had fully recovered and gone back to work. He named my nephew after himself, Derrick Abaho Noble. My mother told me he looks exactly like my brother did when he was little, He is now almost 5 months, and I cannot wait to go back home and meet him.

In October, friends of mine who have a charity in Uganda took a few clothes from me, to my mother and nephew. It is a wonderful connection to think that my nephew whom I have only seen pictures of, is able to wear clothes that I have chosen for him.

It is lovely working here, but feeling homesick is worse than I ever imagined it. There are times when every little thing reminds me of home, and all I want then is just to be there with my family, even when it is impossible.

My mother packed me some millet flour, we often have this to eat at home. I do prepare it occasionally, and I wish I could have it every day, but if I did this, then I would run out of it before the end of the season.

The hardest thing about being far away from home is when the people you love are going through a tough time, and there is not much you can do apart from being by their side, and you are still unable to do that because of the distance.

One of my closest friends from high school Carol, came to check on me before I started my work in Scotland (we had visited each other a few times while we were at University). This time however her voice was different, a bit deeper, and we joked and she laughed saying that "it's a good thing is that it is a romantic voice". Sadly, I was aware that she had been diagnosed with lung and later throat cancer, during this time she lost her voice, and went through several operations. But we could still chat on the phone, and she also made a few hand crafts to keep busy, and to raise some money for her food. It was good that I had friends from the UK, who bought some of her crafts on their charitable trip to Uganda. It was heart-breaking to learn how different she was now, and how much pain she was going through. It was hard to remember that the last time I was with her, we could speak together and laugh about it, but that now she could now only write me a note, which I could then respond to. We also used "Whatsapp". The amazing thing is that Carol stayed strong and still smiled even in pain. Carol died recently, and I wrote this in her memory:

She smiled more than she did anything,
she smiled more than she talked,
she smiled more than she cried,
she smiled more than she judged,
She smiled more than she questioned,
she smiled more than she did anything,
because no matter what Carol did,
she did it all with a smile.
A smile not just for herself but for us who met her,
who knew her and loved her.
Carol never stopped smiling.
We remember to smile, as it is a sign of hope.
Bye for now Carol, smile of hope.

Ever since Tom and I visited Carol at the hospital, my eyes were opened. I have since decided to visit patients at the hospital, even those I do not know whenever I have an opportunity. A few months ago, while I was in Uganda, I went to visit cancer patients at Mulago hospital. I had planned to take a few towels that I had got from Iona, and talk to some of the patients as I know that some people could go a day, or even a week, without a visitor if their family are working, or they are on their own. I also left a little money for food for a few of them, as I felt this was the least I could do. I started inside the hospital where I chatted with at-least five different patients, and as I was about to leave I saw a lady in her 50's laying outside on the balcony, and another girl probably 12 or 13 years old, I had assumed, when I first saw them, that they were sun bathing as it is a beautiful country.

I was shocked however to discover that they had both travelled from Gulu district, and had been waiting outside the hospital to be admitted. They said they had used most of their money on transport and food, and now did not have any more money, not even for even pain killers. I was getting emotional and thought if I cannot be strong on their behalf I need to leave. I left them with the little bit of money I had left, which would help them for a few days.

They appreciated it so much and asked for my prayers. I told them I would pray for them and keep them in my thoughts when I got home. Even as a Ugandan, I had not known how bad the medical situation was in my country until then; I hope we can all join hands to get it better. Every single action counts, you do not only have to offer money, talking with someone could give them hope, take away their loneliness, we can do it!! "For God, and my country".

I was also feeling more homesick this year, because most of my close friends and cousins got married, and I could not be there for their parties.

So, when Miriam and Josh, who have been my friends here on Iona since I returned as a resident, invited me to their wedding, this was very special. Miriam has been a great friend, we have been through so much together, have played games, jokes, had naps, walks, danced, advised and supported each other, said the truth to each other, even when it was hard to do.

She is like a sister to me, this was affirmed on her wedding day when I immediately felt like part of their family and sung the blessing for her and Josh at the wedding. I also signed the register. It was my first time to do this, and was very special. Sometimes we joke about me playing matchmaker for Miriam and Josh, it's good to see that it worked, Josh even said this in his speech at their wedding.

Meanwhile, the toilet project is still progressing and fingers crossed it will continue. I have done several sessions with the guests at the Abbey and McLeod centre where I have been working since April. I was also invited to run a session at Bishop's House, which is another Christian retreat centre on Iona, and this was very rewarding.

Robin, friend and former staff member of Iona Community, left most of her belongings behind after her contract ended. These she donated, and the money raised from them went towards the accessible toilets for children in Uganda. The questions, ideas, suggestions, discussions and generosity that people show are sometimes overwhelming. The world is still a promising place with such people still out there, especially at the moment, where negativity and bad news seem to have taken over across the world. It gives me great hope.

A group of children who visited from London held a raffle. Whoever held the lucky ticket, received a glass of lemonade, and an opportunity to sit at the front row during the weekly guest concert at the centres. They raised £115, and it was moving to see how the children involved were concerned about issues of other children in the faraway continent of Africa.

Dorothea a child of 6 years worked with me on a service of peace and justice, during the service I carried her on my back, together with a Jeri-can of water on my head, through the Abbey Church to demonstrate what it would be like for an African single mother fetching water and caring for her child. Dorothea did not speak much English, but her mother explained everything to her, and helped her to make children's crafts when they returned to their home in the Netherlands where they were able to raise more money to support children with disabilities in Uganda. I wish more children would get involved since this gives us even more hope for a future of people who think these issues are important.

Jan, who is an Iona Community member and poet, also raised money through poetry sessions, came up to me after this particular service and said she would "always remember the powerful image of a precious child on my back, and precious water that is so scarce in many places".

Different volunteers and guests who attended sessions have also returned home and spoken to their families and churches about this project, this has helped spread the word, awareness and raised additional funds.

At the time of writing, we have enough money to construct the toilets in another school. I am hoping to go to even poorer parts of the country when I return, and who knows, we may have enough money to construct toilets in more schools. Also, I would like to offer to sessions in Uganda to talk about the need for accessible toilets, even in public places. In the future if the country, and people involved in planning, can all know the need, each school and public place would hopefully have accessible toilets.

I also hope that the level of acceptance and love for people with disabilities will increase, as for many years they have been left out, even by their own families. Several years ago, they would have been seen as cursed, so things have improved with education, but I wish it would improve even more.

I am humbled by everyone's generosity and support, several times I have been in tears, not just because of the financial support, but because of the genuine concern that people have, and would want the situation for people with disabilities to be better. Lots of people offer their time, to find out as much information as they possibly can and then offer their knowledge and expertise. It is through this that we are able to develop new ideas; for example putting windows in the toilet blocks, which we would not normally have, but someone suggested this would be better for lighting. I will, when I return to Uganda, evaluate the schools where we have already constructed toilets, to see how they are, and also to hope for even better facilities; which I know will possible with all the support and help we are already getting.

One of the roles as a resident staff member here on Iona is leading pilgrimages. This involves at least two first aid trained members of staff, who together with guests walk around the island, stopping at places of spiritual significances and having a short reflection including a prayer and often a song. Some things I have found very significant are:

The erratic boulder

This is made of granite and is not native of Iona; it was carried very many years ago by the glaciers. It has been weathered by different seasons and climate changes but still stands strong.

This is a reminder of to me of how strong we are, no matter what goes on around us, it also highlights the love of God. It reminds me also of the story we were told while growing up, that demonstrates Gods love and Parental love:

> Once upon a time, there was a mother who loved her son so much, but they lived in two different places. The mother lived above her son's house, so she would always look and watch out for him, she would also throw lovely food, goodies, toys anything she thought that the son would like, enjoy. But every time she threw something down, the son would grab it and never look to see who had sent it. This happened several times, and the mother missed the son so much, all she longed for was his acknowledgement, attention, and appreciation or even awareness that she existed. One day, the mother threw a stone instead of a cookie, it did not hit him, but the son immediately looked up, wondering who had thrown him a stone?

They explained to us that most times we continue grabbing all that we can get, but when something unexpected, or difficult happens, it does not mean our parents have stopped loving us, they are still there, and will face this alongside us.

However, we should not take things for granted, we should take time to appreciate what we have already got.

Crossroads

On Iona during the pilgrimage there is a reflection at the crossroads, these are the only crossroads on the island. When we look at them, the roads look like small tracks. Early in the 19th centuries, before internet, televisions, and phones were popular, these would have been a place where people shared information, or even caught up on the island gossip.

We have all at one time or another been at crossroads in our lives; it gets really scary, leaving the familiar and travelling into the wilderness, to what is unfamiliar or uncertain. In my own life, it was not easy to leave the country I was born in, the people I knew, the warm weather, to travel to what I did not know. A different country and culture. I had lots of questions, will I fit in? Will I be accepted? How will it all be like?

Crossroads are a reminder that we do not actually have to always know it all, to have all the answers, but we just have to let what has to be, "BE". We do not have to always be in control.

Also at the crossroads, we learn to step outside our own comforts, and sometimes we end up touching the lives of those around us even unknowingly

When we undertake the reflection at the crossroads, we take a moment to think of times in our own lives when we have been at the crossroads, or people in our hearts whom we know are at a crossroads in life. The last time I did this reflection, a guest from the Iona Abbey came up to me later and said he had a story about crossroads he would like to share with me. I liked the story and later asked him to share it with everyone on the pilgrimage on our way back which he did.

He said:

There was once a man who committed murder when he was a young boy; he was then sentenced to 15 years in jail. On his return, he started joining in services and prayer discussions. One day he said, that he was very angry with God, that his mother as he was growing up had told him that all that happens in his life is written. Why then was he sent to jail; if it was written that he would murder this person, and probably also written in the victim's book that they would be murdered?

This started up much discussion in the group, with anger, questions and wondering.

The next time he came to the group, he put his hand up. He said to the minister, "I know the answer, it is because it was also written that I would be jailed for 15 years".

After this, the man did not come to the prayer group for a long time, and then the minister went to his home to inquire and to see if he was okay. This man told the minister that he was unable to face it all, he was guilty and had sinned, that God had not written all this in his book. He had merely put him at the crossroads, given him choices. He knew now that life was not a straight path, he needed to make decisions.

Later, they both explained this to the prayer group. A member of the group said that "yes, we are put at the crossroads to make a decision, and it does not end there, when you complete that crossroad, you will find on the journey that you are often then given another crossroad, and another new journey".

It was therefore up to him, to forgive himself, and to take another journey.

What I learnt from the story is that if we make mistakes, can we start all over? Can we forgive ourselves? We should not ignore what we did in the past, but we can use it to help us heal and move forward.

When people hurt us or hurt themselves, does it help to blame them? They are probably already blaming themselves; it does not help to add more injury to a wound.

In addition to pilgrimages, it is good to walk with friends. Miriam, Richard, Josh and I do not usually manage to get a day off together, so it is not always easy to organise doing something together, especially if it means getting off the island. After a few failed attempts - ferries being cancelled because of the weather, the weather not being appropriate for a long walk, we finally managed to organise a day on Mull for a walk. Unlike the last time we had walked on Mull together, where I had packed a tuna tin, and forgot the tin opener, this time we all had our sandwiches ready. It was a lovely sunny day, beautiful to see the blue shiny sea, and tall green trees on Mull.

Not far from where we started out, we found a swing, we all had a go. I had forgotten how much freedom swinging gives, and how much I loved to swing when I was little. It feels like being in your own world, full of freedom and peace, not scared of anything. I sung as I enjoyed the swing.

We then carried on with the walk, towards our destination: the Carsaig Arches. We had long wanted to do this, but the road had been closed for a long time for repairs, so this was a good opportunity. We did not have long however and could not risk getting lost (at the time of year we were walking, it gets dark very early). However, we did have a light and enough food and warm clothes, so we were all ready for this, if it did happen. We got to our destination by lunchtime however. It was so spectacular, and I was so glad we made it.

On our way back, from a distance, we saw a £20 note that was wrapped in a water proof bag with a stone pressed carefully on top to stop it from being brown away. As we got closer, Richard picked it and removed the note, only to realise that it was not a £20 note, it was made to look exactly like it on top. On the back of the note there was text from the bible and also the message: "do not be fooled this note is fake but Jesus is real".

We had discussions about it, one said, "it is a bad way of trying to convey Gods message, it makes whoever sees it angry, immediately they discover it is not money, which makes the messengers into liars".

I personally looked at it lightly, and thought someone was trying to make a joke, and had a sense of humour which often gets lost in spreading the word. Most of the time the Christian message comes out too seriously, and that people think that they must be perfect, hating every minute they make a mistake. They forget about being simple, having fun, and realising we can all still learn a lesson, even with a bit of humour. What would have been your reaction? I still wish to discuss this further and hear different views. What lessons could I, or you, learn?

A Third Season on Iona

Life is indeed a journey and the road on Iona has been at times rough, at others calm, with lots of challenges and lessons, but they all have made it worthwhile.

The most important part of working, and living here though, is that it is hard to separate work from the rest of the time when we are not working. I like this because for me work is part of life, and whether we live at the workplace or not, the two are connected. It is more meaningful for me to know that what I would do at my workplace, is what I would like to apply in the rest of my life. This is it what brings me back to the fact that enjoying what I do is very important. One of the practical things that attracted me to work here, after my time as a volunteer, was seeing people who have what are normally big, or important roles, all working together.

For example, seeing Sharon who was at the time Deputy Director, and the rest of the team, washing up together after service teas. I was humbled, and to me, this was a symbol of discipleship, being servants to one another. We need more leaders in this world than bosses. It may not be as good as it should be on Iona, but this kind of "discipleship leadership" is still demonstrated in lots of different ways. I pray and hope it spreads.

As a hospitality team, we all give ideas, and where possible apply them. During the season, I tell volunteers that I am their line manager but that we should always be open to ideas. Possibly knocking down the building and rebuilding it in a day, that would be wishful thinking. But those ideas which are within means, and are practical, we can consider.

Normally people will come up with good ideas to make something that irritates them better. One of the volunteers for example, hated the fact that the kitchen in the Macleod centre got very congested when everyone was trying to set up the tables ready for meals; he hated people coming one by one to wash their hands in the kitchen. So, I asked him what his solution would be. He suggested a sink in the common room, which would reduce the congestion in the kitchen. Later I told my line manager, who took it further, and now this has been done and does make a big difference. People often think that the sink has always been there, or wonder how could it possibly have not been pointed out before.

I suppose what I am saying is that valuing people's ideas, no matter what their position or social standing, would make a big difference to the world.

Would it be possible to put people before power? Is power even necessary?

It does help for someone to take responsibility for making the final decision, since a group of people sometimes take longer to decide, and it can be impractical. But we do not have to be in control of everything. Power can be evil, especially when it is not used for the good of those we lead or serve.

When it comes to the cultural shock of living in a different country, there have been a few shocks for me, having soup is one of them. I did not like soup, but after almost a year of not having it at all, I finally found the secret; peanut butter. If I stir some in, it becomes delicious! We have soup every day for lunch on Iona, so I was glad to have found a way of making it bearable. We often have stew back home, so it has taken quite a long time to get used to soup. I now put peanut butter in my soup, no matter what type of soup it is, and I like it better.

I had been brought up with several cousins, and stayed in shared dormitories in school, often with more than 40 people in one accommodation block. We also had a small house, but I do not remember guests not staying at our home because there was no room. We shared beds, put mattresses on the floor. There is a saying in Uganda, "it is not the bodies that get congested, but the hearts". This is me trying to translate it literally to English - it implies that a room can be packed with many people, as long as they get on, it is not a problem. However, if you put only two people in a big space who do not get on, it is much harder.

It took me a long time to understand why people on Iona needed their own space. I tried to be in their shoes, and look at it from their perspective, thinking it would definitely be different, if they had been brought up with lots of other people, as I had. However, I tried, as much as I could, to respect other people's views, and not to invite lots of visitors into our shared accommodation. When one day I did invite friends to come to watch a movie, and said, "whoever wants to come along please do", I had no idea that it would be so many. I was so pleased, it felt like home, "just come whenever you would like to", and no personal invitation was given.

However, this later caused a lot of upset to the people I shared with; we discussed and talked about how in the future, we needed to send an email, or inform everyone, when we wanted to have visitors around.

I was very upset, mostly because, each of us has a personal room. This is a massive house, and most people were usually in their rooms, with no one in the big living room. It was often empty for a long time with barely anyone, apart from those just passing through once in a while.

Another thing that happened that upset me even more was when one of the staff got into trouble because they had not asked permission before they used the garden. Even when Scotland has a freedom of movement policy, and communal grazing area on Iona. I thought, "how can we say we shall welcome refugees" when we cannot even welcome our own colleagues? Can we offer unexpected welcome if we need to inform everyone in case of a guest? Is this actually what hospitality is?

When you live in a community, it is important to compromise, and talk openly. Later that afternoon, I chatted with one of the staff members about this, she explained to me her views, I explained mine, and by the end of our conversation we had agreed. The best outcome was that I started to understand and got to know this particular staff member even better. A few months later, she became like my own sister.

CHAPTER TEN

REFLECTIONS ON MY JOURNEY

Looking back on my time on Iona several things stand out; the first time I was asked to read in the Abbey Church, which was full of people. I had never even read at church in my own home, so this was scary. The reading, which I recall vaguely, was about women being submissive to their husbands. Several people told me I had read it well, one man however said, "you would think you got that reading straight from Africa, because that is what people do, I mean African men." Zam Walker (an Iona Community member), graciously tried to explain to this man the deeper meaning of the reading, also telling him that the person doing the reading is not the one who chooses the reading. Whether he understood, I do not know!

Then came the time where I was asked to do my first service, I did this with Angela. I was so nervous, therefore instead of reading out the prayers of thanksgiving and concern, I decided to sing them. I knew a song from primary school that worked well, it was easy for me to feel at ease when I was singing.
I sang:

Prayers for thanksgiving:
> Father we thank thee, for the night,
> and for pleasant morning light,
> for rest and food and loving care
> and all that makes the world so fair.

Prayers for help and concern:
> Help us to do, the things we should
> to be kind and good in all we do,

in work, or playground,
to grow more loving every day.

I shared the leaders seat with Angela, and this helped me to have the confidence to do a service on my own the next time. Leading services, and being ministered to, is one of the greatest experiences of being on Iona. Not every service is the same, and they do not all touch us in same way, but when they do it's so fulfilling.

One of the things, that is a blessing here on Iona, but sometimes I find a challenge, is water. It is a great gift to be able to have plenty of water, however I find myself struggling when there is too much waste.

When I first came to the UK, my guardians told me that I could get drinking water straight out of the tap; it sounded too good to be true, so I thought they were joking. Later I realised they were serious, water from most taps is safe to drink in the UK. When I started working on Iona, my friend noticed I was only putting a little water for washing up cutlery in the basin. She would have to top up every time. One of them told me, "you should forget about saving water here because it will not evaporate to Africa, so it does not matter whether you save it or not, you might as well enjoy it since it is there". I was a bit upset at the time, but thought, "they are probably right". However, it also made me try harder to think of other ways of how "not wasting water" could be useful, other than wishfully thinking that it would evaporate to places where they needed it.

During our weekly pilgrimage on Iona, I got an opportunity to explain more about the importance of water, I did this at Loch Stonaig which used to be the main water supply for the Island.

I also led a few services for justice and peace in the Abbey Church about water. I would often explain to people how those who live here are so fortunate to have enough water, while other places in the world suffer, either with lots of water that causes floods, or not much, not even enough to drink. Having experience of living with not enough water myself, even now, when I am at home in Uganda, gave me more courage to talk about it.

I encouraged people to take advantage of the fresh water straight from the taps. Encouraging them not to buy bottles of water, but to just buy a recycling container and put tap water into it, even when taking a walk or on a journey. This could help save some money, then the person would be able to contribute the money saved towards water charities, or even do other things.

After a few months of working on this, Christine (who is my friend and an Iona community member) told me that every time she brushed her teeth, she would think of me, and immediately turn the tap off until she needed to rinse the toothpaste off. This helped me to realise that sometimes you do something and wish it to be taken seriously, but never know if it has been. It was so good to get that feedback and as a housekeeping team on Iona we have also taken a few steps of our own to save water. We use the water that was used to rinse utensils for mopping, cold drinking water left after meals, we use for watering plants. Also, since not many people drink water at breakfast, even though my mum says, "you should, it is good for you", we only put a jug at the front, and refill it if we need to, instead of putting a jug-full on every table.

I know this may never help all of the disabled children who find it difficult to fetch water, or even able bodied people who cannot find water, wherever they are in the world, but I feel it is right to be able to do whatever is within our means to avoid waste.

Chapter Ten

The hardest thing I find on Iona is saying goodbye. It does not seem to get any easier, we just learn to live with it. We treasure the moments we spend with all the wonderful people who come here, and we hope to meet them again at some point, which is often the case since people do return to Iona. Almost every Wednesday we say goodbye to one group of volunteer staff, and then new ones arrive. Fridays, we wave off the guests at the jetty. It does not take long for close relationships to develop on the island and for some reason, friends become really close; like family, then before you know it, it is time to say goodbye again.

During the season, we get to take time off, holidays, where we can do what we like. I cannot really say it is a hobby, but if someone knows me well, they will probably tell you that I sleep a lot. I was on a holiday with my friend Angela, in Cumbria, we had talked the day before about going shopping the following day. Angela waited for me to come for down for breakfast, she waited for lunch, and later she knew it was getting so late that the shops would be closed, so she decided to go shopping. A couple of hours after she had left, I went to the bathroom, came downstairs, put the kettle on and started putting peanut butter on my bread.

Ken, Angela's husband, said, "Dora, do not eat too much, we shall be having dinner soon." I was used to Ken making jokes, so I thought he was just pulling my leg, as I was having my breakfast.

When I looked at the time on the oven however, it was after 6pm and a few minutes later Angela appeared, back from her shopping trip. Surprisingly, I went to bed again soon after 10pm that evening, and I also slept soon after entering the bed. If I have a hidden talent, it would have to be sleeping!

My grandmother says it does not help that when I shared a bed with my mother for several years, she would cover me up and leave me to sleep as she went to prepare breakfast. My mother told me recently that it is because my elder sister, who was Derricks twin sister, suffered from malaria and later died of pneumonia, she was therefore scared that it might happen to me too. She also she realised that I did a lot of work after I had woken up.

When I went home to Uganda recently, I woke up in my own bed, then went to my mother's bed, where she found me some hours later. She said, "going to Iona, being abroad, has turned you into a grown up, responsible person" yet deep inside, I know that I am still her little girl, and Istill think her bed is warmer, nicer!

This year I have met so many more amazing people. I got so close to most of the volunteers, we had so much fun. I learned from them, love, forgiveness, acceptance, being strong.

The most thoughtful card was made for me by Patty, it was a selection of small cards, put in a very beautiful box, all hand made. One said "open now", others: "open when you angry", "when you miss me", "when you need a hug", "when you are having a bad day", "when you feel lonely", "on your birthday", "when you need to know how much I love you", "when you need a good laugh", "when you are homesick", "when you are sick", "open at Christmas".

During her time here we had lots of special moments; when I took Marc and Patty for a walk and we lost our way, we kept going, hoping, and saying "It is just around the next corner." They both hated me, their shoes were covered in bog. However, we had our lunch and lovely conversations as we walked.

Another time, we were on a beautiful beach, when Marc, picked me up and carried me on his shoulder.

He kept saying he was taking me to the sea, and I thought he was joking. By the time that I realised he was serious, he had already thrown me into the sea, had sips of salty water, and the water was absolutely freezing for a cold Ugandan. I hated him, but it was not too bad, just water anyway, so I forgave him.

About a year later, at the same sort of time, there must have been over sixteen people on this beach, I remember being put in a blanket and tossed up in the air. It was so scary, yet so much fun. I cannot fully explain, I felt these two things together, as both scary and fun. I enjoyed it and screamed my lungs out...literally!

Colonsay

I enjoy singing and dancing. Since I have been on Iona, with the help of different people, I have sung more often, even in public, than ever before. I have always loved singing and will always sing anytime that music speaks to my soul. I sing when I am happy, sad, worried, excited, I can express almost every emotion through singing. I can sing at the top of my voice, as if I am the only person in the entire universe when I am taking walks. On Iona, you cannot miss the chance to sing, we sing while washing up dishes, cooking, at services, on walks, anytime and I love it.

A few months ago, Richard, Musician at the Abbey was invited to play the piano at the church in Colonsay, my dad Danny and I joined him for the trip. We could not get there on the first day however, getting from Iona to Colonsay meant getting 3 different boats and they had been cancelled because of poor weather. The next day we managed better; it was a long boat trip however and lasted over two hours. By the time we got there, the weather was much better and we went for a cycle around the island which was spectacular.

Reflections on my Journey

On Sunday, the church was holding a service about music from around the world. I was therefore invited to sing, and did this in my own language. I enjoyed it, and as on many small islands, lots of people knew each other and were very warm to visitors. They stopped us as we went about, and greeted us, it was a great weekend. The time spent with my dad and Richard was also wonderful, cooking and watching the sunset. We even managed to even cycle to another nearby island, where there was an old Abbey. It was soon going to be Miriam and Josh's wedding, so with seaweed, we worked together and managed to draw a beautiful heart in the sand. We used the image later to make a card for their wedding. It was a very sandy beach, with sand-dunes too.

Richard and Danny could cycle faster than me, however I kept to my own pace and sung my heart out. It was heart-warming, and I enjoyed it so much, and sung songs that I had not sang in a while.

Every Monday evening on Iona, we have a ceilidh, which is a Scottish social gathering where people meet for Scottish country dancing, and to perform poems, or jokes, in between the dances. From the first time I had danced this way, when I first visited Scotland, I have enjoyed them. It does not matter what gender your partner is, you do not have to be a dancer, you just have to enjoy dancing. You just grab a partner, and dance like no one else is watching. This is often my highlight of the week. The weekend we were on Colonsay coincided with the island's music festival. Richard and I went down to the village hall to check on this, but decided that as it cost a lot of money to buy tickets, and the weather outside was beautiful, that we would dance outside, which we did for almost an hour - it was great! A few people were outside watching us. They must have thought we were crazy.

Perhaps I should have a ceilidh at my Ugandan wedding? Who knows! Maybe a band would be complicated, but I could organise a CD, not too bad after all!

Some of the treasured memories from this year: my friend Leone, from Germany who loved reading stories. She started reading me bedtime stories, I felt so spoiled, it was wonderful. Almost every night, Leone, would come to my room sit by my bed, and read me a story, as soon as I fell asleep, she would switch off the lights, and leave gently for her room. Once she even came with a friend Matthew, then Eleanor and they read in turn. She must have read to me for more than two months, this was so special. I do not remember bedtime stories growing up. I suppose with a paraffin lantern it would not have been safe anyway, so this was a nice way to catch up. She was such a kind, warm hearted, talented girl, she shared her time and I will always remember and treasure it. We would chat about life, homesickness, food, dances, love life, singing, anything, just before she started reading the stories. She definitely lit up my year.

Every Friday at the centre meeting on Iona, we share the "highlights", "wow moments", or what made us feel "so alive during the week", and also what the challenges have been. Writing this book, and reviewing the whole of the past twenty-six years of my life is not the same. There are lots of wows, lots of challenges. I wish I could share more of them, but I do not even recall what they are. I am not known for having a great memory, after all I almost usually live in the moment. Enjoy the moment, hardly worry about the future, and forget so easily, but I am pleased that I have been able to recall all that I have. I never thought I could do it, when I started writing.

If you have been to a place you loved, enjoyed, grew in different ways, you would understand it is quite normal to want the people you love to visit this place. For those that have not been to Iona, it is a beautiful place, it is hard to explain exactly what goes on here on Iona to someone else, except wish they could be there themselves.

I would wish most people in Uganda could visit Iona, it transforms you, you learn so much, but most of all I would wish Tom could visit Iona.

We tried to arrange for him to visit, but twice his visa has been denied. The Visa and Immigration Agency said that this was because they could not trust that he would go back to Uganda. Also, the Iona Community does not know him personally, only knows him through me.

Every time we tried, I would be optimistic, he would have as much evidence and references as he could, once he had over fifteen reference letters, I still have a note of all of them. It is unfortunately, hard to build trust, especially with other people misusing their visas. This means that the ones who genuinely want to visit also lose the chance, like the rest they cannot be trusted.

Also, we did not have enough money to prove that he would be supported without using public funds, which was another reason for denial of the visa. However, I hope someday we will both be able to visit.

When Tom did not get his visa, it was disappointing and sad for me, people supported me, wrote cards, said encouraging words and gave me time and space to cry it out too. I got several cards but this was really special and helped me so much:

> Hi – I heard the news yesterday that Tom's visa didn't come through. I am sorry that he did not get

it and I know you are very sad about this, broken hearted.

I just want to tell you something and that is how nice it is to know and to see you and to work with you everyday. You are a calming presence with your singing and dancing and laughing. You are a good example to me of what is important in life...people.

I hope when you check your pigeon hole and find this card that some of the pain has subsided a bit. I know I can speak for everyone here when I say that we love and cherish you.

We have a saying in a different fellowship I belong to, "This too shall pass." I need to use it when things get hard, it may be helpful for you.

All my love,

It could be 40 years from now. I will not lose hope, this place that has taught, challenged and blessed me through so many people and memories. It would be worth sharing it with my Tom.

On Iona, every Wednesday, there is a guest concert, people do acts such as, plays, songs, poems, clean jokes, play instruments, it is a wonderful time spent together, having fun.

My two favourite jokes that I have learned from these events are: "I wondered, why the baseball was getting bigger and bigger........ Then it hit me". This I learnt from Steve, he knows over 200 jokes, most of which I cannot easily understand why they are funny.

The next one is a bit long, almost like a story:

Once upon a time, during the depression, a gentleman was looking for a job. He tried looking for jobs everywhere in vain, he decided to go to the zoo and inquire if there were any vacancies. To his disappointment, they said there were no vacancies. However, the manager said they had just lost their monkey, if he did not mind, he would be offered a job as a monkey. He would need to wear a monkey costume, and stay in the zoo, and would be paid according to however long he was at the zoo as a monkey.

He was already tired of job hunting, so there is no way he would decline this generous offer. He soon started his job, and would put on his costume, climb the trees, eat bananas jump up and down a few times as a monkey would do.
They got more and more tourists due to all the entertainment from this monkey.

One unlucky day however, as the monkey was trying to entertain people high above in a tree, a branch fell off that he was leaning on. Below him, was a giant lion, that opened its' mouth and roared at him. Very scared he screamed, "Help! Help!"

The lion responded, "Shut up, or they will fire both of us!!"

Amongst the many amazing things of working on Iona, is getting to know the guests; working alongside them in the kitchen and serving each other on the tables, like a family. We sing as we wait for the dishwasher, dry up, set up tables, it is great fun. It is a privilege to do the kind of work that I enjoy, and I do not take it for granted.

Getting to know people happens even faster on the weeks when there are fewer guests, for example, during work week, where people agree to come to help do the jobs like spring cleaning, painting and decorating, and helping to get the centres ready for the winter closure. During the last winter work week, we played a joke on one of the staff members. Natalie, really liked double cream, so when dessert was served, with cream, I took the cream off the table and hid it just next to me. In a few seconds, my neighbour had passed it on to the next person, and the next person. By the time I looked to end the joke, it had gone almost around the table, I enjoyed it. Everyone was cooperative, and happy laughing, something simple like hiding a dish of cream, had made everyone on this table a team.

Some of the guests who come for the work week, like Jim, have also been coming for years and years. They are therefore at home when they return. Jim, in particular, also likes playing jokes. On his recent stay, he put two signs on staff office doors. One of the staff, the director, had just been away for a holiday, so when she came back to see, "office closed in preparation for painting", she believed it.

Then the other office (the bookings office) had a sign on it saying, "mattress storage". Natalie, who was supposed to be using this office at the time, was not impressed and wondered how they could think she would be able to work in a small office with the addition of mattresses. She quickly went up the stairs to ask those concerned, only to discover that it was a joke. These moments, make guests and staff build friendships, well, after they have got over the effects of the practical jokes.

It is so rewarding, to see guests coming every week, hear people say their lives have been transformed. Some of the groups from the under privileged areas of Glasgow, seem to often be the most generous, and are grateful for every little thing. The experience on Iona means so much to them, and even without a lot money, they make crafts, cards, buy chocolates and appreciate the work from the staff. We have a lot to learn from them.

I recently read an internet post about a blind man who stayed all day on streets. He had a note and a box, the note said: "I am blind please help me." Several hours passed and there was just a few coins. Another man passing asked if he could change the wording on the note. He rewrote it, it now said, "it is a beautiful day out there, and I cannot even see it". After that many people started putting money in his box. He wondered just what the man had written. Later in the day when the man returned, the blind man was able to ask him what he had written. He told him, and that both notes showed other people he was blind, and the box meant that he needed help, but the second note acted as a reminder to people of jut how fortunate they were, at being able to see a beautiful day. Sometimes we are too busy worrying about what we did not get right, what is going to happen in future, lost in wishes, and we forget to appreciate what we are so fortunate to have in the present moment.

Iona is a place where it is easy to fit in for most people, rather like Paddington bear did when he got to London. Last year someone asked me how it feels to be the only black person on staff, or the whole island for most of the time.

I responded with, "am I black? Yes, I am actually black skinned, but the important thing is that people here do not make me feel black."

People on Iona are really accepting, and do not discriminate, they value people for who they are, not just what society labels us to be.

Marc from Catalonia Barcelona, who was a volunteer and now a good friend, told me during his first days working with me in the housekeeping teams, that one of the many reasons he had come to the UK was to improve his English.

He came up to me one day after the toast had been burnt, he could not recall how to say the word burnt.

If you are not a native English speaker, you can easily understand those moments when you know what you would like to say but ca not figure out the English word for it.

He therefore said to me, "Dora, this toast is black, I will throw it away." I turned to him and responded, "do not be a racist!"

He did not know at first whether I was joking or serious. I have not experienced any racism here, and of course I was joking. I wonder whether I would have been able to make this joke, or whether he would have been able to describe the toast as black, if there was even a simple sign of racism here? How would it have been in a place where there is racism I wonder? The joke would have probably been taken seriously, because it would mean that you throw away whatever is black, because it is seen as less value.

One of my closest friends is gay. As a person who grew up in a place where if anyone was gay they were discriminated against, tortured, expelled from school. I have learned a lot from him.

We have talked a lot, and he has told me about his fears as a gay Christian. He has wondered whether he can serve God and still be gay? He wonders if this hurts his parents, family, friends. He has found it hard to reveal that he is gay. He was fearful, would people still accept him, would he accept himself? I asked him if he minded me writing this, he was pleased that I was.

All of this often makes me ask: can Christians accept people for who they are, without judging? Can we spread more love instead of discrimination? I know there are a lot more questions that have come up in so many churches following same topic which some have increased divisions.

But if the greatest commandment is love? How can we claim we obey it if we discriminate against our brothers and sisters? How could we help more people to be believers?

Even if I did not know that it is okay to be gay, I do know what is not okay, and this is discrimination, hate, oppression, injustices and together we can fight against what we know is not okay.

Iona is a place where people come from all over the world, sometimes just on the staff team we have people from more than twelve countries and those with different accents, cultures etc. I hope for a day when racism, segregation, discrimination of any kind will come to an end in the bigger world. People will be accepted for who they are and not left out due to labels put on them by society.

During staff training two years ago, we visited Glasgow, and spent some time with the Iona staff members based there, and also with members of the Iona Community. Whilst there, we had an interesting Glasgow pilgrimage led by community member Alison Swinfen, who told us mainly about her concerns for asylum seekers, and her daughter Rima who used to be an asylum seeker herself. We had an opportunity to stop in Nelson Mandela street where the youth workers working for the community continued to tell us more about "People, Politics, Poverty" in respect of inner city regeneration, and how this affected young people.

It was all great information, and some of the stories were really touching. It is amazing seeing what the Youth workers had been doing, and gave me hope for a future where the younger generation is involved. The Youth Festival is held every year on Iona, and both the McLeod Centre and Abbey are filled with so much life, noise, laughter, singing, challenges, hot chocolate, and learning from each other and of course from the, "adults" also there.

Each year there are different themes for their programmes, but what touches me most is seeing how the young people who come want to live out their actions, not just for one week, but even after they have left Iona, and how they also start discovering and believing in themselves more. (It is hard to imagine such a large amount of growth happening in just a week).

This year the theme, was "speaking truth to power". The leaders encouraged the young people to remember that nothing can stop them from acting, living their dreams and visions. Not even their young age should stop them. They proved this by encouraging them to participate in services, speak in public, tell their stories, being involved at the guest concert. Freedom, love, acceptance and encouragement filled the building.

Iona is not a very big island, most locals know each other and can usually tell who is a day tourist, an Iona Centre staff member, or a guest staying at one of the Iona centres, or the hotels. During the busy summer, people meet in different places; the pub, Parish Church, Catholic House of Prayer, Bishops House, on walks, at the Spar shop, post office, GP surgery, village hall, jetty, or on the ferry. There have also been so many lovely organised events that bring the local people who live on the island, and those who are on the island for a little while, such as film nights.

A regular memorable event for the past few years has been the "ladies' meals" at the Columba hotel. This happens once a year and started many years ago, but not of course going back to St Columba's arrival!

During these meals, we have had great conversations, and Sister Jean, from the Catholic House of Prayer, tells wonderful jokes, really, really, funny ones. For me, that is always the best bit of the meal.

Joining in with the "island choir" is also fun, there was one time when both the Iona and the Mull choirs went across to Staffa island. We sang in Fingals cave. The sound of the music through the cave, together with the waves of the sea, was unbelievable. We also enjoyed the lovely food and great views on the boat back.

Another event that brought people together even though it was the first time that it had happened - it even made the national newspapers, was this year's turning on of the Christmas lights that were decorating a large Christmas tree that had been made out of fishing creels'. The evening was splendid, lots of drinks, I had hot chocolate, one of the best ones I have had so far on Iona.

The primary school children singing and performing drama, is also wonderful. This year we shall be singing Christmas Carols with them in the parish church with parents and Iona Centre staff, it will be a great moment.

To me, it does not matter how hard we try to be independent, think we can do it all on our own. We are naturally dependant on each other; we need each other as much as we need God. This is also because God manifests himself through people. Loving those people we meet in our daily lives, proves our love for God.

ACKNOWLEDGEMENTS

It has been a few years since I started thinking about writing, there have been a few times when I started, but did not finish. In 2016, several people inspired me to start writing again. Some of them asked whether I had a written story about the toilet project that started from Iona two years ago. It was because of this encouragement from other people that I thought, "maybe I can give it another go". In fact I did write a short story which was published in the Iona Community magazine (Coracle) about this in 2014 and in the SECMA (The Scottish Episcopal Church Mission Association Magazine) in 2015.

One day however I was in the pub on Iona jetty, looking around to see if Danny (my dad) who was planning to visit me on Iona, had arrived when a lady who had been a guest at the McLeod centre where I work, greeted me saying she had just been telling my story to her friend.

She said that she had been wondering whether she could write my story, she explained that she was a writer in her home country, Netherlands. However, after we had talked, her friend said to her "no", and told her "Dora needs to write her own story". I kept thinking about all of this and wondering if it was a sign that I had to write about my life.

A few weeks later, I heard about the film, "Queen of Katwe", it had been filmed in Uganda, and was about a girl born and raised in Katwe a slum in Uganda, but had become a chess champion, which had changed her life. A book had been published about her story. This was another inspiration.

I later went to the Cinema with Sarah, who is a friend and has been involved with a charity based in Uganda. There were only three other people watching, and one of them, the wife, was born in Uganda. It was a lovely experience, I laughed, cried, smiled, wondered, and sang along most of the songs in this film. I was so inspired.

I started writing a few pages which Edmonde (who is like an Iona mum) read. One of my closest friends Richard also read what I had written. I wanted to know if the words, the sentences, actually made sense? They both encouraged me to go on.

I finally spoke to Sue Dale, an Iona Community member who is also a writer, and said she would guide me, even encouraged me to continue writing whatever I can. Sue was my final inspiration.

Lightning Source UK Ltd.
Milton Keynes UK
UKOW04f1212140817
307265UK00002B/419/P